LUNA

TAMARA DRIESSEN

LUNA

Harness the
Power of the Moon to
Live Your Best Life

PENGUIN LIFE
AN IMPRINT OF
PENGUIN BOOKS

PENGUIN LIFE

UK | USA | Canada | Ireland | Australia
India | New Zealand | South Africa

Penguin Life is part of the Penguin Random House group of companies
whose addresses can be found at global.penguinrandomhouse.com.

First published 2020
002

Copyright © Tamara Driessen, 2020
Illustration copyright © Carmen Seijas Rosende, 2020

The moral right of the copyright holders has been asserted

Set in 13.5/16 pt Garamond MT Std
Typeset by Jouve (UK), Milton Keynes
Printed and bound in Great Britain by Clays Ltd, Elcograf S.p.A.

A CIP catalogue record for this book is available from the British Library

ISBN: 978-0-241-41813-0

www.greenpenguin.co.uk

Self-awareness is your superpower

CONTENTS

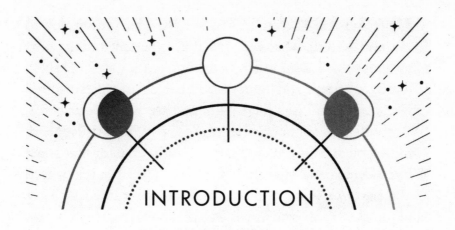

INTRODUCTION

What are you going to write on your list? I was sitting with my housemate at the kitchen table talking about the things we wanted to release and say goodbye to, with a little help from the last full Moon of 2012. At the top of my list, I'd written the name of an ex-boyfriend I'd split up with earlier that year; even though I was moving on, there was still something that wasn't easy to shake. You know that feeling, when life seems to be getting back on track, then their name's brought up, or you bump into them unexpectedly, and you're struck by a tidal wave of emotions *again*. I was ready for a fresh start. The best thing that came from the relationship (or the end of it, at least) was that it catapulted me onto my spiritual healing path. I guess you could call it my 'awakening'. They say that everyone who comes into our lives is a teacher: he woke me up to the fact that the situations I kept finding myself in were a reflection of my self-worth, or lack thereof. It was time to start doing things differently.

My friend and I wrote our lists: first, what we wanted to let go, and second, what we wanted to experience in the next twelve months. I went to my bedroom, got my abalone shell, White Sage bundle and lighter for a Native American inspired smoke-reset ritual (see page 149), and we put on our coats. 'What will the neighbours think of us?' We both laughed. Huddled outside in the cold, armed with a lighter and some White Sage to make sure that the ghosts of the last year stayed in the past, we burnt the lists of what we wanted to leave behind, then took it in turns to smoke-cleanse each other, making sure there wasn't any energetic debris still attached to us from what we'd released. We were standing under the full Moon, surrounded by a cloud of smoke. 'Let's use the smoke for the new-year lists to make sure they're blessed, too.'

I left my crystals in the garden to charge under the moon-light and we went indoors to warm up with a cup of tea. Back at the kitchen table, I shuffled my Goddess Oracle cards and spread them in front of me. With my eyes closed, I ran my fingers over the deck until I connected with my card for the year ahead. I pulled it from the deck to reveal an Egyptian goddess, Sekhmet, saying, 'You are stronger than you think you are, and your strength ensures a happy outcome.'

If you'd told me then that I'd go from working as a hair-dresser to becoming a full-time healer, Tarot reader, author, leading Moon ceremonies and teaching people to connect with crystals and the Moon around the world, I wouldn't have believed you.

How did I know that the ritual had worked? Well, everything on the list became reality. It wasn't until I bumped into my ex at a festival and thought about it a few weeks later, that I realized, 'Oh, yeah, I saw him and it didn't bother me at all.' It wasn't a *thing* any more. I was officially over him. I'd also been in recovery from a long-term eating disorder, and I'd written on my intentions list for 2013 that I wanted to cultivate a healthier relationship with food. My guilt around food and body shame was diminishing, with the support of weekly therapy sessions. I know it's a total cliché but, slowly, I was learning to be more comfortable with myself.

Since that evening, Moon rituals have become a regular part of my practice and so many of the things I've manifested, like this book you're reading now, my first book *The Crystal Code*, my partner, the house we live in, being part of an incredible community, the challenges I've overcome, can be attributed to a greater understanding of the Moon, with my other spiritual practices. It's come from consciously observing the Moon, the way I feel at each phase of the lunar cycle (see page 29), which zodiac sign it's moving through (page 47), and acting on the intuitive nudges that I get from doing the work.

The ancient science of astrology can help us to navigate the pitfalls of modern life, and a quick peek into what the stars are saying is only an app away. The Moon is one of the celestial bodies that is visible to us, which makes it easy to study its cycles and access its power. It's about more than just moon-gazing and being in awe of its presence: more and more people are aware of its influence on their moods and energy levels, and are interested in its powers for healing and transformation.

The gravitational pull of the Moon affects the tides. Humans are made up of 60 per cent water (depending if you've drunk enough today): is it such a stretch of the imagination to consider that the Moon can also influence us? According to astrology, all of the planets govern different aspects of our human experience but, here, we're going to be talking about the Moon.

Getting to know the Moon is like nurturing a long-term relationship: the more time you devote to it, the deeper you can go, the more wisdom that's revealed to you. You may see old patterns that have been keeping you stuck, or discover ideas and desires buried under a lot of 'shoulds' or realize when it's time to move on (hello, eclipse season!).

Feelings aren't facts but they can reveal a lot. You've got the answers already within you; the Moon can help you find them.

The Moon was an object of worship for ancient civilizations. There are sacred Moon temples around the world, such as the Aztec Pyramid of the Moon in Mexico, the Temple of the Moon in China and Somnath Temple in India. Myths of lunar gods and goddesses are woven throughout history. The 'Triple Goddess' symbol, depicted with a waxing, full and waning Moon, represents the feminine stages of maiden, mother and crone. It has been associated with mysticism, and witches, Wiccans, pagans and shamans, who have been celebrating the Moon for centuries and harnessing its powers. Its personality is often described as maternal, Mama Moon, its cycles linked with rebirth, nourishment, intuition and mystery. It guides us towards introspection. The Sun is said to illuminate our conscious mind while the Moon encourages us to dive into the subconscious.

What we'll explore in this book isn't a trend, it's a way of life. We're just going back to our roots: once upon a time humans used to live more in harmony with the universe. If we can find the sweet spot between listening to our intuition, embracing our innate cycles and living in harmony with nature, alongside the perks of modern living, then we could be on to a winner.

People often become interested in the Moon because they want to get in on the manifesting benefits it can offer. Who wouldn't want support to make their dreams come true? You could think of setting intentions with the Moon, like new-year resolutions but with more power. The Moon seems to amplify intentions, especially when they're spoken in ritual or ceremony with a group. The phases of the Moon are an opportunity to check in with where you're at and make your own magic.

At one of my Moon ceremonies, someone said, 'It's so nice to be surrounded by people who want good things to happen for you, when the city can feel so lonely.' It isn't lost on me how privileged we are to be able to come together like that. I've seen friendships blossom between people who've met at ceremonies: they've arrived as strangers and left feeling understood by the other person because the rituals have revealed that they've been going through similar experiences. It's incredible what can happen in two hours. There's so much power in finding you aren't alone, especially when you're moving through feelings of self-doubt, crisis, trauma or uncertainty.

There's so much more to the Moon than just setting intentions and hoping it's going to bring us abundance in all shapes and forms. It's like throwing a penny into a wishing well: we can't resist the temptation to do so because *what if* your big dreams could happen for you? Communing with the Moon is an opportunity to ask for what you want, especially when you don't feel as if you can ask in some of the day-to-day aspects of life or you're losing faith in your current situation. The Moon is always there to listen.

The Moon guides us to turn our gaze inwards, to understand our motives and that the guru we're looking for has been there all along. The Moon is a mirror, and helps us learn to decipher what we need, especially when life gets crazy and overwhelming. Self-care is more than just a hashtag: it needs to be non-negotiable.

It's reported that more people are experiencing stress, anxiety and depression than ever before. I speak to so many who are feeling the pressure, with not enough hours in the day or days in the week to achieve everything they have to do. The result? Your work life creeps into your personal life where you're replying to your manager at 10 p.m., and it's the last thing you do, just before double-checking that your alarm is set for the morning. As soon as you wake up, you're checking your emails so that you can get ahead of yourself. Eat, sleep, scroll, repeat. What happened to our boundaries, people? I think that people who actually work nine-to-five, keeping the rest of the day for themselves, are like unicorns. Mythical creatures. And this isn't just about those of us who work: if you're studying, a parent or caregiver, this applies to you as well. I can't remember the last time I spoke to someone who felt they had this juggle totally locked down.

I hope this book will act as a permission slip to those who are on a well-worn path to burnout to take a break, because you need it. If you're reading this book, I'd say you're here because you're getting the call. The call to start trusting your intuition. The call to start trusting yourself. The call to learn how to love yourself more. The call to create more balance and space to catch your breath. The call to remember and discover what makes you happy. The call to start believing that you deserve more. The call to be unapologetically you. The call to feel less alone and be a part of something. And those nudges ain't going nowhere.

It might seem totally counter-intuitive to take time out to meditate or do a ritual when you've got a million and one things to do. However, when you do the things that recharge you, or simply allow you to be in the here and now – even if it's only for ten minutes a day (to start with) – it can magic-ally make time expand. When you're relaxed and centred, your mind will be clearer and it's easier to focus on what needs doing, rather than being reactive and perhaps making avoidable mistakes. A chilled you is more likely to think of creative solutions to problems that will make life seem effort-less. With any luck, following some of the suggestions in this book will guide you to get to know that ultimate version of yourself a whole lot better.

You don't need to buy a ticket to the other side of the world to find yourself: follow the Moon and see where she takes you.

HOW TO USE
THIS BOOK

You might read this book from start to finish, or flick through to see what your Moon sign says about you and your loved ones (see page 81). Perhaps you'll dip into it on the days when something's in the air that you can't quite put your finger on and you want to see what the Moon is up to, or when you're planning your rituals. Use the Tarot spreads when you're looking for clarity. See what comes through as you put pen to paper with the Moon sign journalling prompts (see pages 56–79). Write notes, highlight sections you want to remember, fold the corners of the pages to mark where you're at, add Post-it notes of quotations, intentions, observations and sigils (page 217) that you've created. I encourage you to *do* these practices to bring it all to life. This book is here for you.

Some of what I share you'll relate to, and if you track your cycles and energy, you'll find your own patterns and points of tension. Trust them. That's your internal compass. Rather than feel you have to apply what I'm sharing with you to every aspect of your life, choose one area, or something you'd like to manifest. Energy flows where attention goes, so you'll find this effective and less overwhelming.

Remember: you don't need fixing. This is all about you getting to know yourself, cultivating emotional intelligence, practising self-care, learning to go with the flow and living a life that feels in alignment with your values.

Your Moon magic, or witchy abilities, is not determined by gender, sexuality, race, religion or cultural background: it is open to all.

Come as you are; you don't need an invitation. You belong in this coven.

• • • MOON DIARY • • •

In this book you'll be introduced to the Moon and her phases, alongside astrological associations. Feel free to use them as a guide, but I encourage you to keep a Moon diary so that you can get to know how the Moon makes *you* feel, act and think. It could be as simple as having a designated journal to record the day, Moon phase, Moon sign, where you are in your menstrual cycle (if applicable), and what's been coming up for you. Of course, there are Moon apps (at the time of writing this The Moon is my go-to app but there are others that I haven't familiarized myself with yet) you could use to track and note what you're experiencing. Another thing you can do: at the end of the day, use your smartphone's calendar and note some emojis that reflect your mood, interactions, inspirations. With some consistency, you'll be able to see the patterns as your energy waxes and wanes. I'd recommend tracking your energy and observing how you feel during the Moon's phases: see how each one resonates for you. There are wellness apps you can use to log your moods and energy levels. It usually takes three to six months to see a pattern so it's worth being as consistent as you can in inputting your data.

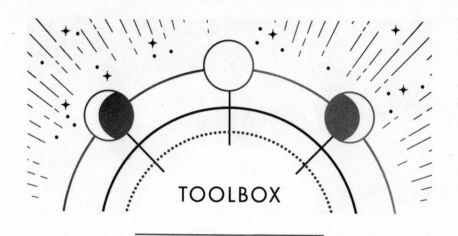

TOOLBOX

Journal: a dedicated notebook to write your heart out and record any lunar insights and epiphanies (learn more about journalling on page 131).

Tarot and/or oracle cards: working with these is an opportunity to check in with yourself and see what the energy forecast is saying for you (to learn more about Tarot and oracle cards, see page 155).

Crystals and minerals: act as an anchor to help you align with an intention or give you some support or protection when you need it.

• • • CRYSTALS AND MINERALS • • •

I like to think of crystals and minerals as cosmic life coaches: they all have their own perspective and 'advice' to help you feel supported and call back your power. Trying to work with several crystals at the same time may confuse the signals you get from them, especially if they represent very different intentions. You may have ninety-nine crystals but you need only one, as long as you're making the time to get to know it and see your life through its lens and guidance.

Crystals and minerals can work through a process called entrainment (when a person synchronizes with an external influence that affects how they feel, act and move). For instance, when you hear a song that instantly shifts your mood, makes you want to dance or you can't help but sing along, that's entrainment in action. Crystal healing works on a subtle level, which is why it helps to meditate, practise rituals, sleep with and keep them close by so that you can align with their energy without too many distractions.

Crystals and minerals have found their way into the mainstream; at the time of writing it's an unregulated industry. This means that the people who are mining them may not be working in safe conditions (with hazardous health implications), are possibly underage and aren't being paid adequately; they may also be having a detrimental impact on the surrounding environment. Make sure that your crystals have come from sustainable and ethical dealers. Don't be shy about asking the person you're buying them from if they've been sourced responsibly.

Try not to be sucked into spiritual materialism. More crystals don't equal a fast track to enlightenment or manifestation. It's what you do with them that counts.

Tip: Put your crystals out to charge under the Moon to give them a boost!

Salt: Dead Sea, Epsom or Himalayan for baths. You can improvise with kitchen salt if you need to.

Flowers and herbs: for ritual baths (see page 242) and smoke-cleansing rituals (page 145). Dried flowers and herbs are better for smoke-cleansing rituals and also have a longer shelf life: you can keep them on standby for whenever you need them.

Heatproof bowl and self-igniting charcoal discs: for smoke-cleansing rituals.

Candles: for ambience and Moon rituals.

Essential oils: harness the essence of flowers, herbs and roots; the oil carries the plant's scent and healing power. These fragrances act as plant medicine: they can elevate our senses. I prefer to use organic essential oils so that I know they aren't mixed with anything synthetic. *Please check to ensure that it's safe and suitable to use specific oils for any particular purpose.*

Apps: we're increasingly on our phones so we may as well use them to get to know ourselves better. I'd recommend using an app to track the Moon cycle and signs so that you can stay informed with what's going on in the sky; a wellness app to track your energy levels, moods, sleep and overall health so that you can observe any patterns; and a menstrual tracking app has been a game changer for me.

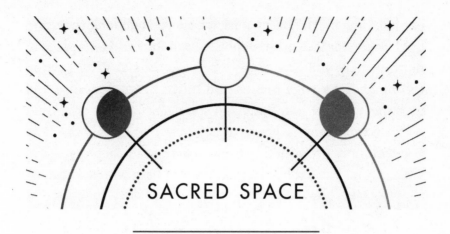

SACRED SPACE

You don't have to take a pilgrimage to a holy site, pray in a church or worship in a temple to feel connected with your spiritual self. You don't need to affiliate with any kind of religion (unless you choose to) to feel held in or create a sacred space. A sacred space is a sanctuary. It's a place for communion, whether it's with your highest self, the Moon, Mother Earth, the universe, God, other deities, your spirit guides, ancestors, crystals, or within a circle of trusted people. It's where you don't have to pretend to be someone you aren't, you can drop any masks you've been wearing and know that you're accepted, just as you are. It's a place where you can just be, surrender and process whatever is coming up for you and be present in the now.

Your sacred space could be at home, perhaps your bedroom if you're living in a shared house, or sitting in front of your altar (see page 224) or in your favourite armchair, where you meditate or simply sip a cup of tea as you look out into the garden, or even the bathroom, where you can lock the door, light your candles and soak in the bath. It could be a place in nature where you love to go when life feels as if it's getting too much, or a yoga mat as you move through asanas and reconnect your mind, body and spirit. Perhaps it's attending a Moon ceremony or going to a retreat. All of this can help you feel more grounded but, ultimately, your sacred space is within you. The external situations can help you land there.

YOU TIME

Make time in your schedule to be in your sacred space: if it's scheduled (and non-negotiable) it's more likely to happen. You could plot the Moon phases in your diary and block out some time to do your Moon reflections and rituals. Book the Moon ceremony, yoga class, workshop, retreat, massage, healing treatment, life-drawing class, date night with your beloved, brunch with your best friends, a family visit, a day off or a holiday. Arrange a baby- or dog-sitter, if you need to. Ask your partner to pick up dinner on the way home. Cancel an outdated obligation. Say no (kindly) to the frenemy, who's always take, take, take. Give yourself a digital curfew and switch off your phone so that you aren't getting sucked into a work WhatsApp conversation when it's way past your bedtime.

If you know that you need some solo time at certain points in the month/Moon cycle/menstrual cycle or time to decompress after a big event or family get-together, book the time out in your schedule, if you can. And don't feel guilty about cancelling plans at the last minute if you aren't in the mood to go out. You'll thank yourself for it afterwards.

In case you've been waiting for a permission slip, this is it.

Think of time in your sacred space as if you were a phone recharging. We need to prioritize charging our own batteries.

HOW TO CREATE A SACRED SPACE AT HOME

Put your phone on flight mode or in a drawer, make sure that you won't be disturbed or distracted, close the door and soak up some you time. You could tidy up, put some fresh sheets on your bed, light a candle, use your favourite incense or essential oils, do the smoke-cleansing ritual (see page 145), wear something comfortable that makes you feel incredible, do one of the rituals and/or oracle spreads you will find in this book, immerse yourself in a ritual bath (page 242), pour yourself a nice drink, meditate, practise yoga or read a book. You don't have to do all of these things to create a sacred space: choose one or a few of these suggestions, whatever feels good for you.

Tune out to tune in.

A MODERN WITCH

Whenever I mention that I'm a modern witch, one of the most common responses I hear is 'Are you a good or a bad witch?', usually from cynics with a hint of sarcasm. Ultimately, witchcraft is nature-based and worships the Earth, honouring it as our Mother, Healer and Goddess.

The last time I typed 'Witch meaning' into Google, the definition that came up was 'A woman thought to have magic powers, especially evil ones, popularly depicted as wearing a black cloak and pointed hat and flying on a broomstick', and 'an ugly or unpleasant woman'. If you ask me, those are patriarchal ways of demonizing women and totally misrepresent what the craft is all about. I've met a lot of women who identify as witches and they've all got hearts of gold. The thought of harming someone would never cross their minds.

A witch is someone (not specifically female) who is intuitive, a healer, an empath, an activist and a revolutionary. A witch lives by their own rules or is realizing that living by other people's standards isn't working for them. A witch is in tune with their sexuality. A witch embraces what makes them unique. A witch is doing the work, taking responsibility for their life and the impact they have on the world around them.

Wicca is a recognized religion most commonly associated with witchcraft. While some Wiccans practise witchcraft, others don't want to be associated with it. Some people consider the Wicca label more 'respectable' because of its religious associations.

Some witches' practices are rooted in tradition, while others take the eclectic route, cultivating a unique practice that takes inspiration from their heritage, experiences and beliefs. Some worship goddesses or fairies, and others recognize nature and the Earth as living spirits. Some are in covens and others are solitary. Some are hereditary witches, and others were perhaps initiated into witchcraft by a cool aunt, a colleague or someone they found scrolling on Instagram.

We are so privileged to be able to explore these practices and belief systems freely. We stand on the shoulders of so many people who were persecuted and killed for doing what we do. Practising witchcraft was banned for at least two centuries. Doreen Valiente, one of the most influential figures in Wicca, played a major role in having the ban lifted on 29 July 1951. These days, more and more of us are coming out of the spiritual closet and embracing our inner witch without having to look over our shoulders.

To learn more about witches and witchcraft, I recommend reading: *A Witches' Bible* by Janet and Stewart Farrar, *Witch* by Lisa Lister, *Everyday Magic* by Semra Haksever and *Craft* by Gabriela Herstik.

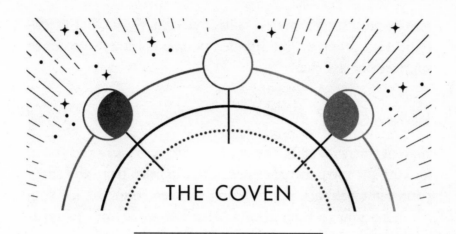

THE COVEN

Historically speaking, a coven is a group of thirteen witches who meet regularly to practise witchcraft and honour the sabbats (festivals according to seasons) and esbats (celebrating the Moon). Sabbats are holy days for witches: they celebrate the passing seasons and are believed to be a potent time for calling in abundance. Esbats are timed to channel the energy of the Moon for casting spells, rituals, manifestation, divination and reflection. Witches are some of the OGs (slang term for original gangsters and originators) when it comes to working with the Moon.

A true Wiccan coven has a specific structure with training programmes, trained priestesses and priests. It's a group of like-minded people with specific roles who come together because the power of rituals and spells is amplified when performed as a collective.

Nowadays, the coven can mean many things, like a WhatsApp group with your best witches, an online community of female entrepreneurs or a collective of activists, but essentially it's a group of like-minded people coming together to support one another.

Joining a Coven

If all of this witch talk has sparked some curiosity and you're looking for a structured organization to learn from and share your witchy experiences, joining a coven might be for you. It's important to keep in mind that being part of one takes work and dedication. It's a way of life.

When it comes to the craft, community is important. This doesn't mean you have to join a coven tomorrow (unless you want to), but is a reminder of how healing it is when we surround ourselves with people who understand us and want to see us doing well. It's all about choosing collaboration over competition, with a much-needed emphasis on diversity and inclusivity. We're all witches in progress. Let's keep raising each other up.

For those who prefer to do things at their own pace and keep things more casual, you could attend either local Moon ceremonies or gatherings that are related to the sabbats. You can form your own witch support group with your friends, even if it's just you and your best friend to start with. Choose which lunation will support you with your goals and get together for some Moon magic.

Remember: we aren't here to convert or persuade other people to get involved. Preaching is usually the quickest way

Abandon the cultural myth that all female friendships must be bitchy, toxic, or competitive. This myth is like heels and purses – pretty but designed to SLOW women down.

Roxane Gay

to turn people off. Always keep an open-door policy and people will join you, if/when they are ready.

Digital Covens

With a little help from the internet, you can also sign up to online sabbats and esbats, which makes them accessible to nearly anyone with a good internet signal. There are membership platforms where you can take part in online Moon ceremonies and spiritual development with ongoing support.

Don't let location hold you back: if your best friend lives on the other side of the world, why not meet via Skype or Face-Time for a long-distance Moon ritual? Arrange the details and what you'll need beforehand, and make some magic when the Moon is right. (See How to Create Your Own Moon Ceremony, page 198.)

You don't have to do this alone.

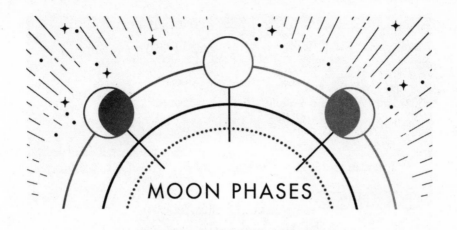

MOON PHASES

Other than astrologers, most people acknowledge only the full Moon (because we all know what an attention-seeker she can be when it's her time to shine) and perhaps the new Moon, but other phases keep things flowing, especially when we follow them.

Understanding the influence of each Moon phase can bring you a deeper awareness of what may support you at different points of the lunar cycle. We're cyclical beings, but with artificial light, busy lifestyles, career pressures, social lives to keep up with, and living in concrete jungles, many of us are fairly removed from nature's rhythms and our own. There can be so much pressure (often self-imposed) to maximize productivity in every aspect of life. Living life as if it's linear isn't sustainable because there isn't any balance. Learning how to pace yourself and slowing down to synchronize with the Moon's rhythm is one way to catch your breath and do things differently.

• • • THE FACTS • • •

- The Moon is a satellite that takes approximately twenty-seven days to orbit the Earth, while the Earth orbits the Sun.
- You can see just one side of the Moon: as it orbits the Earth it rotates on its axis at the same time.
- The Moon rises and sets, like the Sun, but fifty minutes later than it did the day before.
- The alignments of the Moon, Sun and Earth are in constant motion.
- Depending on where the Moon is during the cycle, the Sun's light is reflected by the Moon's surface; this is how we can see it.
- The Moon's phases are caused by rays of sunlight hitting it at different angles during the transit.
- No matter where you are in the world, the Moon phase is the same. So, if it's a full Moon and you're in England, the Moon is also full in Mexico, Australia, Africa, Thailand and Canada.
- The Moon has eight phases: new, waxing crescent, waxing/first quarter, gibbous, full, disseminating, waning/third quarter and balsamic/dark.

For anyone who thinks this is all a bit woo-woo, garden-ers and farmers have coordinated planting with the Moon phases for centuries because it can benefit yield. As the Moon's gravitational pull causes the tides to rise and fall, the moisture content of soil is also said to be affected. It's beneficial to plant seeds during a new or full Moon in the same way that you would set your intentions (see page 33): moisture is pulled to the surface and can boost plant growth. It's also recommended to fertilize plants during the waxing Moon and remove weeds when it's waning. At the turn of the twentieth century, artificial fertilizers were introduced and organic practices were sidestepped in favour of some-thing that seemed more efficient. After a while the deteriora-tion of crops and soil quality became noticeable. Moon-phase planting was rebranded as biodynamic agriculture, which enriched the soil and stimulated plant growth with sustain-able, organic and lunar practices. Working with nature brings better results, not just for the plants but for us humans, too.

Each phase of the Moon brings its own effects, and by understanding their benefits, you can learn how to ride the waves, rather than swimming against the tide. It's a bit like familiarizing yourself with rush hour: you know what to expect so perhaps you give yourself extra time to get where you need to go, use an alternative route or mode of transport, leave at an entirely different time to avoid traffic or decide to stay at home. It's like the Universe's traffic lights, show-ing us how to stay balanced. You may find you feel more at home and grounded in one particular Moon phase. Recent-ly, I've found that I feel exhausted around the time of the full Moon and when it's new I'm more focused; a few years ago, I noticed I would feel downhearted and anxious during a new Moon. When you're aware of how you feel at different times of the Moon cycle, you can make allowances for what's coming up and act accordingly, perhaps keeping your schedule light if you know that at certain points you're more likely to feel overwhelmed or tired, not making plans to be sociable on days you may feel agitated, but booking job interviews, public-speaking engagements or photoshoots when you're more likely to feel confident and outgoing.

NEW MOON
New beginnings; setting intentions;
starting something

This is the first phase of the Moon cycle. The Moon is positioned between the Earth and the Sun. With the Sun behind the Moon, it's backlit and appears invisible from Earth. The new Moon inspires new beginnings. It's a time for reflection and introspection, checking in with how you'd like to move forward. You could think of it as sowing seeds. What would you like to achieve, create, overcome, release or feel? You may feel your energy levels are low so try to avoid rushing. Work with this phase to start new routines, habits or regimes. As the energy of the Moon builds towards full, it can boost your intentions to become part of your everyday life.

In astrology terms, each new Moon falls in the corresponding zodiac sign. For example, if the Sun is in Aries, from 21 March until 19 April, the new Moon during that time will be in Aries. Each zodiac sign will bring different themes to the new Moon and you can use each new cycle to focus on different aspects of your life (see pages 55–79).

WAXING CRESCENT
First steps; increased energy; get planning

After the new Moon, we see a faint glimmer of light that grows into a crescent over the next few days. The waxing crescent represents taking the first steps towards bringing your intentions to life. You may notice that your energy levels gradually increase as the Moon 'grows'. For new projects, this could be the planning phase, when you start to research or update your CV and apply for a new job.

WAXING MOON / FIRST QUARTER
Take action; get things moving;
create opportunities

The first quarter Moon occurs a week after the new Moon and a week before the full Moon. Remember the intentions you 'planted' during the new Moon? This is where you activate them. It's time to walk your talk. *Gently* put your foot on the accelerator to get things moving. Start reading a book that may help you take things to the next level, work with a coach, learn a new skill, go to a workshop or networking event, say yes to that date, embrace the interview you applied for, open a new bank account for your savings and make your first deposit. Break it down into tasks that are easy to action so it doesn't feel overwhelming. Remember: small steps become big changes.

GIBBOUS
Take it to the next level;
higher energy; expansive

Almost full, but not quite. The Moon appears bolder as it reflects more of the Sun's light. This can feel like an expansive time, without the intensity of the Moon at its peak, which isn't too far away. You may notice that your energy levels are rising even higher as the Moon grows stronger. How are you supporting your intentions with your actions? This is a time to build on what you have already been doing and take things to the next level, if possible.

FULL MOON
Abundance; celebration;
reflection; intensity

The full Moon brings a time of illumination, abundance, celebration and culmination. Think of a nectarine, when it's ripe
and juicy. You bite into it and it's sweet and refreshing but at
the same time it can also be messy and sticky. Life can seem
amplified during the full Moon: you may feel you're slaying
it but challenging aspects may also be highlighted. You may
be more aware of external influences and how they affect you:
be kind to yourself (and others) if you feel triggered. It's likely
that emotions will be running high for others – it's not just
you. This can be an intense and overwhelming time.

Depending on which zodiac sign the full Moon occurs
in, certain aspects will be under the spotlight (see page 50).

Use this time for divination, reflection: you may find that
the insights you receive are more creative and guide you
towards taking action. Reflect on what you've learnt, overcome, achieved and manifested. It's a potent time for practising gratitude. Full Moons are thought to be auspicious
occasions to launch new projects or ventures. Put yourself
out there with this cosmic boost!

DISSEMINATING
Slow down; decompress;
breakthroughs

The full Moon may have felt like a rollercoaster, but as it subsides the disseminating Moon is like a lunar invitation to catch your breath, decompress and slow down. A full Moon hangover is common and you may notice yourself feeling more introspective. You may also feel relieved as the energy begins to ease after the Moon has peaked. It's time to process the revelations and breakthroughs or breakdowns that came with the full Moon. Harness this phase by allowing yourself to be more receptive and supported. There's still work to be done but the focus is on tying up loose ends and ironing things out.

WANING MOON / THIRD QUARTER
Declutter; cleanse; let go

In the words of Elsa from *Frozen*, 'Let it go, let it go, let it go.'
Let go of the past to create space for something new because
we're coming to the end of the cycle. The waning Moon
is the time to be casting 'banishing' spells: say goodbye to
exes or frenemies with a cord-cutting ritual (see page 246).
You could also use this phase for reprogramming outdated
thought processes, getting support to overcome an addiction or self-destructive habit. To honour this, you can also
channel Marie Kondo and donate/declutter/recycle/return/
throw away anything that doesn't bring you joy. Clean your
home and perform a cleansing ritual to release any unwanted or stagnant energy.

BALSAMIC/DARK MOON
Direct attention inwards;
low energy; stillness

The last seventy-two hours of the cycle: the Moon continues to wane until it's in total darkness. Regardless of how clear the sky, the Moon isn't visible at night because it rises and sets with the Sun during this phase. The dark Moon is often considered the void. The unknown. The space in between, not quite the end and almost the beginning of a new cycle. Introverts may feel at home during this lunation: it's the time to tune out of what's going on around you and direct your attention inwards. You may find your energy levels lower during this time so plan your schedule accordingly. Get comfy and cosy. This can be a deep time for introspection. Any insights revealed may have depth: you may realize, for example, how you are holding yourself back. You may find it harder to exert yourself but, rather than giving yourself a tough time for not being as productive as you think you *should* be, surrender. You're exactly where you need to be. Keep things low key and simple. The dark Moon could be seen as the dark before the dawn: the new Moon is just around the corner and you're likely to notice your energy begin to rise again.

. . . And the cycle continues.

ECLIPSE

Eclipses are a supercharged time, when the Moon's power is believed to be more potent. They occur four to six times a year and come in pairs, solar (new Moon) and lunar (full Moon) eclipses, one after the other. An eclipse can be partial or total, depending on the alignment and how much the Moon blocks the Sun (solar eclipse) or the Earth blocks the Sun's light (lunar eclipse). Whether it appears as partial or total varies depending on where you are in the world at the time of an eclipse. Eclipses can be catalysts for big change and transformation, whether you think you're ready for it or not. Expect the unexpected. Be prepared for epiphanies and truth bombs. There can be an element of turmoil as you're forced into upheaval. If you've wandered from your path and become distracted, eclipse season is there to get you back into alignment. Eclipses can mark a turning point. Think accelerated personal development and soul growth. Life can feel ultra-intense during an eclipse, so give yourself plenty of space to process what it may bring up for you before you take any kind of action. Use this time for reflection; eclipses can reveal the root of what's been holding you back and unrealized potential, but you need to create space for these insights to download. The results of rituals performed during this time can be unpredictable so be careful what you wish for.

Buckle up your seat belt. Even if it doesn't feel like it, you've got this.

Solar Eclipse

Solar eclipses only happen during a new Moon. During a solar eclipse, the Moon is between the Earth and the Sun. The Moon briefly 'blocks out' the Sun and causes a temporary solar power cut. When we are disconnected from the Sun's energy, we may experience an awakening. It may uproot what's familiar to us so that we're forced to see things from another perspective. The universe may be cruel to be kind. Remember that this is happening *for* you, not *to* you. It is guiding you towards higher ground and aligning you with your fullest potential.

Lunar Eclipse

Lunar eclipses happen during a full Moon. At this point, the Earth is perfectly sandwiched between the Sun and the Moon. The Earth blocks the Sun's light and the Moon reflects refracted light from the Earth's atmosphere, instead of directly from the Sun. As we look up at the full Moon at night, the Earth's shadow makes the Moon seem to turn red, brown or grey; this can last for up to two hours. Shadowy thoughts and feelings may be amplified during a lunar eclipse; it's time to practise radical self-acceptance. How can we love ourselves more, practise compassion and release judgement? No more hiding the truth from ourselves. This is a potent time for realization and breakthrough during this turbo-charged illumination.

SUPER-MOON

The Moon's orbit around the Earth is elliptical, which means that the distance between the Moon and Earth varies. A super-Moon (a.k.a. perigee Moon) occurs when the Moon is at the closest point in its orbit to Earth, which makes it appear super-sized in the sky. There are also micro moons (a.k.a. apogee-syzygy moons), when the Moon is furthest from the Earth and appears to have shrunk. A super-Moon may occur during a new or full Moon and isn't uncommon. You may notice that the characteristics of the lunation are amplified during a super-Moon.

BLUE MOON

This doesn't mean that the Moon turns blue: when two full Moons occur in the same calendar month, the Blue Moon is the second full Moon of that month. These don't happen often – 'once in a Blue Moon'. It's believed that a Blue Moon hosts an amplified connection to spiritual energies. You can collaborate with a Blue Moon to focus your intentions on something that has seemed unattainable or unlikely, until now.

BLACK MOON

When two new Moons occur in the same calendar month, the second of that month is called a black Moon. It usually happens just once every two and a half years. Due to time-zone differences, the month that a black Moon occurs can vary. In 2019 the black Moon occurred during July for the United States, and August for the United Kingdom. There are mixed views on what it signifies: some astrologers say that a black Moon has no astronomical influence and is just like any other new Moon; some witches believe it has amplified cleansing energy, which can be like a soul purge to release any skeletons in the closet that have been holding you back (subconsciously). At this time you may feel as if you're being pulled backwards. What could you release from your past that may lighten your load and set you free? This enlighten-ment may fast-track your manifestation process.

*

To collaborate with the Moon, I suggest using the phases as a guide to what action to take and when. When you lean into each phase, there's no room for anxiety because you know you're exactly where you need to be. You could think of the Moon as your mentor, guiding you towards making the most of the entire spectrum of human experience, not just the parts we actively seek, like fun, joy, pleasure, achievement and success, but discomfort and uncertainty. It's all part of the process.

MOON NAMES

Ancient cultures from around the world have given the full Moon different names inspired by the behaviour of the animals, plants and weather during each month. The names can give you an insight into what some cultures associated with each of these full Moons.

MONTH	ENGLISH	CELTIC	WICCAN	ALGONQUIAN	CHINESE
January	Old Moon	Quiet Moon	Wolf Moon	Wolf Moon	Holiday Moon
February	Wolf Moon	Moon of Ice	Storm Moon	Snow Moon	Budding Moon
March	Lenten Moon	Moon of Winds	Chaste Moon	Worm Moon	Sleepy Moon
April	Egg Moon	Growing Moon	Seed Moon	Pink Moon	Peony Moon
May	Milk Moon	Bright Moon	Hare Moon	Flower Moon	Dragon Moon
June	Flower Moon	Moon of Horses	Dyad Moon	Strawberry Moon	Lotus Moon
July	Hay Moon	Moon of Calming	Mead Moon	Buck Moon	Hungry Ghost Moon
August	Grain Moon	Dispute Moon	Corn Moon	Sturgeon Moon	Harvest Moon
September	Fruit Moon	Singing Moon	Barley Moon	Harvest Moon	Chrysanthemum Moon
October	Harvest Moon	Harvest Moon	Blood Moon	Hunter's Moon	Kindly Moon
November	Hunter's Moon	Dark Moon	Snow Moon	Beaver Moon	White Moon
December	Oak Moon	Cold Moon	Oak Moon	Cold Moon	Bitter Moon

MOON SIGNS

DAILY MOON SIGNS

As the Moon orbits the Earth, it moves through the twelve zodiac signs and transitions into the next sign every two and a half days. The Moon influences us every day in different ways. You may wonder why some days it's easier to perform certain tasks than it is on others: one day you're super-focused and productive but the next you're restless and easily distracted. Use your understanding of how each Moon sign can influence your mood, like a weather forecast. In a similar way to checking the weather, you can look up which zodiac sign the Moon is in for some clues as to what to expect during that time (see pages 55–79). At the beginning of the month, you could use your Moon app to jot down the daily Moon signs in your diary and reflect on your plans. It may help you to get the best out of situations or choose auspicious days for setting dates. You needn't cancel or postpone appointments if

the Moon sign seems less favourable on a particular day, but keep in mind the undercurrent, use that awareness to your advantage and be prepared.

When I learnt about the daily Moon signs, it blew my mind. I went back through some dates that were notable to me, like a photoshoot, which had been super-easy. The Moon was in confident Leo – no wonder I'd felt so relaxed in front of the camera. On another shoot day I'd felt really self-conscious and couldn't get into the mood: the Moon was in introspective Cancer. And then there was the day when I took a situation personally and cried about it for hours: hello, Moon, in emotional Pisces.

While I've been writing this book, I've been utilizing the Moon signs to help me go with the flow. I booked a place in Margate as a writing retreat. I thought it would be an idyllic place for the words to flow but I didn't consider that the Scorpio Moon was better suited to the crystal healing workshop and full Moon ceremony I hosted there: the Moon's mood was reflective and transformative, rather than creatively expressive.

Just as you'd check the weather forecast to see what to pack for a holiday, or if you need to take an umbrella with you as you leave the house, use the Moon forecast to get the best out of a situation. You could use this information to help you plan an event, an ideal time to pitch an idea to your boss or to schedule a self-care day: in some Moon signs you'll find it easier than in others to switch off and recharge. When we're conscious of the varying factors that influence us, we can use them to benefit us instead of feeling we're up against it.

Each Moon sign will be nuanced, depending on other planetary alignments, and I'd recommend tracking your moods, experiences, productivity and motivation each day. There are lots of mood-tracking apps – for example, Daylio and Moodtrack Diary – but you could simply add some emojis on your phone's calendar that relate to what you've experienced that day.

NEW AND FULL MOON SIGNS

There's usually a new and full Moon once a month, unless we have a blue or black Moon (see pages 43–44).

Every new Moon falls in the sign of a zodiac season: for example, a new Moon in Leo occurs during Leo season (22 July–22 August). Every zodiac sign has an astrological mirror, also known as a polarity. The zodiac wheel has 360 degrees, and the polar opposite sign always opposes the other at 180 degrees and there's six months between them. The mirrored signs have a yin and yang effect: they're (polarized) very different personalities but they're also complementary and balance each other. You know what they say: opposites attract. This means that two weeks later the full Moon will fall in the opposite sign: if it's a new Moon in Leo, the next full Moon will be in Aquarius. And six months after the new Moon in Leo, there will be a full Moon in Leo.

It can take six months for the intentions that you set on a new Moon to manifest, and you may see things culminate on the corresponding full Moon. On the new Moon in Taurus

(2019), I led an online Moon ritual via Instagram Live and my friend Pip attended, using a piece of Pyrite for the crystal healing activation. Collectively we set our intentions for the new Moon: Pip was looking to open her own yoga studio and wanted to use the ritual to support the process. Fast-forward six months to the full Moon in Taurus, the day that the fitting-out was completed on Now Studio and Pip was ready to open the doors to her community.

This is one of the reasons why I recommend keeping a Moon diary so that you can record everything and observe your progress. It's nice to be able to have proof of what can happen when you set your Moon intentions, or the manifestations and magic might go under the radar.

Sometimes manifestations can happen sooner, and there are times when they don't come to life at all: trust in the process and timing. If it hasn't happened (yet), remember that if you asked for something better (see page 191), something else may be on its way to you. If you've got a strong attachment to what you're calling in, loosen your grip. Surrender. You could use one of the waning Moon rituals (page 246) to release any attachments to outcomes and create some space for what you'd like to happen in your life.

What is meant for you won't pass you by.

• • • RECAP • • •

Each new Moon corresponds with the zodiac season in which it falls, and two weeks later, the full Moon will be in the astrologically mirrored sign. New and full Moons don't happen on exactly the same day but they always align with the same zodiac seasons every year. Please consult a Moon calendar or app for accurate days and times.

21 March–19 April: Aries season
New Moon in Aries/full Moon in Libra

20 April–20 May: Taurus season
New Moon in Taurus/full Moon in Scorpio

21 May–20 June: Gemini season
New Moon in Gemini/full Moon in Sagittarius

21 June–22 July: Cancer season
New Moon in Cancer/full Moon in Capricorn

23 July–22 August: Leo season
New Moon in Leo/full Moon in Aquarius

23 August–22 September: Virgo season
New Moon in Virgo/full Moon in Pisces

23 September–22 October: Libra season
New Moon in Libra/full Moon in Aries

23 October–21 November: Scorpio season
New Moon in Scorpio/full Moon in Taurus

22 November–21 December: Sagittarius season
New Moon in Sagittarius/full Moon in Gemini

22 December–19 January: Capricorn season
New Moon in Capricorn/full Moon in Cancer

20 January–18 February: Aquarius season
New Moon in Aquarius/full Moon in Leo

19 February–20 March: Pisces season
New Moon in Pisces/full Moon in Virgo

It is so liberating to really know what I want, what truly makes me happy, what I will not tolerate. I have learned that it is no one else's job to take care of me but me.

Beyoncé

HOW TO USE THIS SECTION

Just like daily Moon signs (see page 47), the zodiac signs bring a different flavour to all of the new and full Moons. You could think of the zodiac wheel as a curriculum for personal development and the signs as dynamic teachers. Each new Moon is the beginning lesson, bringing an opportunity to reflect on and cultivate different aspects of your life as you navigate through the cycle. By the time of the full Moon, six months later, you could be reaping the rewards of the work you began at the new Moon.

In this section you'll find a guide to the daily Moon signs (also known as Mooncast), each new and full Moon according to the twelve zodiac signs, and journal prompts to help you reflect on the specific Moons. You can do this alongside one of the Moon rituals (see pages 217–256), the corresponding Moon phase oracle spread, or create your own Moon ceremony (see page 198).

 Recommended crystal to work with this Moon

 Planet associated with this zodiac sign

  Element associated with this Moon

ARIES MOONCAST
Headstrong; assertive; determined

When the Moon is in this sign, people may be convinced they know best (yourself included), and it may be tricky to find the middle ground. This energy is great for feeling bold and starting new projects, but when it comes to teamwork, there's a chance you could end up locking horns. Instead of challenging authority, be mindful and strategic in the way you introduce your ideas. There may be a sense of impatience in the air. Don't give in to the pressure, especially if you aren't ready.

NEW MOON IN ARIES
Taking action; feeling bold;
brave and new beginnings

Journal prompt: If I knew that I was fully supported I would . . .

Take some overdue action and say yes to whatever lights you up. Less procrastination equals more manifestation. When self-starting Aries is aligned with the new Moon, it can bring a fresh dose of optimism and you may notice a boost in confidence. Focus on setting intentions and committing to the things that will help you do things your way. It's time to be your own cheerleader.

◈ Amethyst
🔥 Fire
● Mars

FULL MOON IN ARIES
Being under the spotlight; ambitions; recognition and expansion

Journal prompt: What has challenged me over the last six months? What have I learnt and how can I do things differently to take things to the next level?

Make some moves that are going to upgrade your life. Dare to dream big. No one knows what you are capable of (including you). Rather than focusing on what you can't do, channel your energy into what you can do and work out how to turn your challenges into game-changing opportunities. Don't be shy about talking up your achievements and promoting yourself. If you've been dimming your light to fit in, this fiery full Moon will pass over the mic so that you can show the world exactly what you can do.

◈ Garnet
🔥 Fire
● Mars

TAURUS MOONCAST
Stability; security; stubborn

Taurus can be stubborn so this isn't the ideal time to initiate new ideas: whoever you're pitching them to is likely to want a guaranteed outcome before they commit. You may find yourself drawn to being in nature and craving open skies, especially if you're in the city. The hustle can seem less important during this time. It's all about finding the balance between working hard and indulging yourself. This sensual sign adores food and the finer things in life: book a table at your favourite restaurant or plan a date night. It's a good time to practise self-care.

NEW MOON IN TAURUS
Practicality; commitment;
grounding; security

*Journal prompt: What new habits can support me
and how will they benefit me?*

Create habits that are going to give you lasting results. Forget the fad diets or get-rich-quick schemes. Slow and steady wins the race. Be clear on your goal and break it down into small (realistic) steps. Just think: if you do one thing every day for the next year, those 365 actions will undoubtedly make a difference to your life. You could open a savings account with monthly standing orders, give yourself goals to aim for at work, or set some targets with a friend to help you stay accountable. It's the small steps that add up to the big shifts.

◈ Rose quartz
⛰ Earth
● Venus

FULL MOON IN TAURUS
Money; stability; nature; sensuality

Journal prompt: I love my body because . . .

Get in the slow lane and tune into what you need. If your self-care practices have fallen by the wayside, now is the time to take care of your body. Make sure that you're getting enough sleep, drinking enough water and doing the things that nourish you. Make pleasure a priority. Indulge yourself. When was the last time you let someone treat you (for a change)? Practise being receptive and allow things to come to you. When was the last time you asked for help or support? Being stubborn might be keeping you stuck. This full Moon can put money and our values under the spotlight: use it as an opportunity to affirm the ways that you're abundant and (re)focus on what's important to you.

◈ Malachite
⛰ Earth
● Venus

GEMINI MOONCAST
Fast-paced; distracted; dynamic

If you sit still for too long when the Moon is in Gemini, you may find yourself easily distracted and restless. As much as you might want to take it easy and recharge, lie-ins and slow, lazy days are unlikely during this time. Gemini rules communication so if you've been on the lookout for inspiration, use this energy to brainstorm, collaborate with like-minded people, and innovate. This dynamic energy is ideal if you're in sales, public speaking, teaching, writing or making new friends. These days are light-hearted and expansive. People may be chattier than usual: try not to get caught up in gossip.

NEW MOON IN GEMINI
Education; personal development;
networking; collaboration

Journal prompt: Write down all of your ideas and the things you'd like to learn about: which ones are you going to make happen over the next six months?

Tune into your next big idea. One of Gemini's themes is communication: do you feel you're being heard and seen? If not, how can you change that? You could use this new Moon to reflect on how you want to collaborate with others. Gemini can be chatty and sociable so there's an emphasis on broadening your network. Sign up to a course, start reading the personal-development book that's been gathering dust on your bedside table, go to a talk or workshop, and catch up on a documentary that will expand your mind.

◈ Kyanite
◎ Air
● Mercury

FULL MOON IN GEMINI
Change; upgrading technology; conscious communication; intellect

Journal prompt: How can I be more honest with myself and others?

Expand on everything you've been learning, whether it's from working with the Moon and personal realizations you've had or in a professional or educational capacity, and how you're going to implement it all. The cosmic forecast could read gossipy: don't get caught up in conversations that you'll only feel bad about. Channel this full Moon to ensure you're using your voice to make a difference. Pay attention to what you're saying: words are like spells. What we say can influence us so much more than we realize. If you catch yourself saying something limiting or judgemental, get creative with those words and see if you can reframe them in a more expansive and compassionate way.

◈ Galena
◎ Air
● Mercury

CANCER MOONCAST
Emotional; supportive; reclusive

As the Moon moves through Cancer, you may feel you're riding a rollercoaster of emotions. Take some time out to do what nurtures you. Most importantly, reach out and ask for support: you don't have to go through this alone. If you've noticed that someone has been quieter than usual, don't take it personally. If you're concerned, don't be shy about checking in to see if they're okay. When the Moon is in Cancer, you may be drawn to spend more time at home and make it feel like a sanctuary. It's a good time to cultivate healthy boundaries and give yourself permission to take a step back if you're feeling overcrowded and overwhelmed.

NEW MOON IN CANCER
Home; emotions; security; faith

Journal prompt: What nourishes me?

Make sure your home feels like a sanctuary and give yourself space to experience all of your feelings. You might find yourself more emotionally sensitive than usual: have a good cry or do something that will help you release some emotional energy, like reiki, yin yoga or boxing. Or is it time to find a good therapist? You could focus your new Moon intentions on things and actions that will make you feel more secure and cultivate more trust in your life.

◈ Moonstone
◆ Water
● Moon

FULL MOON IN CANCER
Hygge; togetherness; appreciation; wellness

Journal prompt: What makes me feel safe?

Set some boundaries and practise forgiveness. The full Moon in Cancer might make you feel nostalgic and sentimental, or cause you to feel triggered by someone who hurt your feelings but you never spoke about it. Tread carefully: this can be a time of heightened sensitivity. How can you respond or share how you truly feel rather than reacting unconsciously? This Moon can highlight what makes you feel safe, including financial security: perhaps this is a good time to open a savings account. If not now, then when? Even if it's just a small percentage of your earnings, it all adds up.

◈ Mangano calcite
◆ Water
● Moon

LEO MOONCAST
Attention-seeking; confident; open

If you're naturally shy or introverted, your confidence may be boosted when the Moon is in Leo, which allows you to be more comfortable receiving attention. This can be beneficial if you have a photoshoot or interview, a public-speaking engagement, or are hosting a party. It's all about self-expression and sharing your truth: think of a lion roaring. Egos can be like peaches during this time: easily bruised. Be mindful in the way that you communicate.

NEW MOON IN LEO
Passion; leadership; desire; pride

Journal prompt: I'm passionate about . . .

Tune into how you can take the lead. Don't wait for opportunity to come knocking on your door: make it happen. This lunation could have you craving more action and adventure. Check in with how often you say yes to things you don't want to do against what brings you joy. You need to put yourself in the way of inspiration. It's unlikely to find you while you're scrolling on the phone or hunched over a laptop. Get fired up about what you really want and go for it.

◈ Carnelian
♦ Fire
● Sun

FULL MOON IN LEO
Attention-seeking; drama; confidence; good times

Journal prompt: What am I proud of and how can I share the love?

Amp your confidence and speak up for what you're passionate about. You might notice that you're wearing your heart on your sleeve and have a strong desire to tell people how you feel. If you aren't getting the attention and adoration you're craving, it could trigger some insecurities. Remember: it isn't *all* about you. How can you channel your big-heart energy into being generous to yourself and others? Share the glory (rather than trying to steal the show).

◈ Golden topaz
♦ Fire
● Sun

VIRGO MOONCAST
Organization; tidy; perfectionist

Keep meaning to colour-code your bookshelf and get your life/home/business organized? The Moon in Virgo is the one for this. It's all about attention to detail and getting projects finished. Being practical and methodical is likely to come easily during this time. Perfectionist tendencies might be activated so don't give your inner critic too much airtime. Keep your boundaries in mind or you may burn yourself out.

NEW MOON IN VIRGO
Well-being; organization; efficiency;
attention to detail

*Journal prompt: How are my perfectionist
tendencies holding me back?*

Tidy up, declutter and get some systems in place so that you've more time for self-care. You'll most likely be feeling those back-to-school vibes. What have you been putting off until the perfect moment? The time is now. The settings don't have to be perfect: you just need to be methodical. This stabilizing new Moon can help you put some well-laid plans in place. Virgo is health-conscious: you may feel the urge to nourish yourself with wholesome food and movement to elevate your well-being.

◈ Green calcite
⛰ Earth
⬤ Mercury

FULL MOON IN VIRGO
Listening to your body; self-care; boundaries

Journal prompt: What have I achieved?

Start recognizing your hard work. It's too easy to lose sight of how far you've come. You may be more aware of your boundaries (or lack thereof), and that you're giving too much to others. Use what isn't working to help you decide what will support you and how you want to move forward. This can also relate to your diet and how you're nourishing your body. If you haven't been practising any kind of self-care, you may notice old thought patterns are triggered. Be kind to yourself. Loosen your grip on everything you've been trying to control and give your inner critic the day off (until further notice).

◈ Black moonstone
⛰ Earth
⬤ Mercury

LIBRA MOONCAST
Peace; harmony; forgiveness

You may find yourself seeking more balance in your life when the Moon is in Libra. This peace-loving sign brings a dose of harmony so it could be easier to forgive and resolve disputes, as long as the outcome is fair. This is a time when people may be more approachable and cooperative. Watch out for those rose-tinted glasses and check in with your 'why' when making big decisions. You may be swayed by people-pleasing tendencies or over-romanticizing. Being sociable is likely to come easily, and you'll appreciate being around art and beauty.

NEW MOON IN LIBRA
Seeking balance; relationships; creativity; equality

Journal prompt: In which areas of my life am I craving more balance?

Take time to pause and reflect. This new Moon could have you craving more balance and inner peace. If you're feeling conflicted with something that your intuition is trying to tell you, it's likely you're over-thinking it rather than taking a leap of faith. It's time to take responsibility for your decisions, rather than letting other people call the shots. Romance may be in the air, and Libra's harmonizing influence can put an emphasis on relationships and revive those warm, fuzzy feelings. If you aren't in a relationship, you may be tempted to sign up to some dating apps.

◈ Opal
◎ Air
● Venus

FULL MOON IN LIBRA
Equality; decisions; harmony; beauty

*Journal prompt: How can I bring more
balance to my relationships?*

Create more balance in your life. When we're busy, stressed and overwhelmed, self-care is often one of the first things to be made redundant from the to-do list, but we need it to keep us feeling connected. You could use this full Moon as a reason to pamper yourself (not that you need one). You may find that you get fired up about equality: educate yourself and listen to other people's opinions (keep it diverse) so that you can establish your own. Being an activist in progress is better than no progress at all.

◈ Citrine
◎ Air
● Venus

SCORPIO MOONCAST
Intense; impulsive; intimate

The mood can feel intense when the Moon is in Scorpio: you may find yourself deep-diving into conversations you weren't expecting to have and your emotions could catch you off-guard. You may find yourself craving intimacy but at the same time preferring your own company. Situations and other people's actions may trigger your insecurities, and there's a chance you may obsess over a comment that you can't let go. Take a step back and a few deep breaths before you react. This is just showing you the areas of your life that need TLC. You won't be the only one feeling this way so don't fight crazy with crazy. A little bit of compassion can go a long way. Use these days to work on things behind the scenes: reflect, research and refine your master plan.

NEW MOON IN SCORPIO
Power; sex; money; jealousy

Journal prompt: How do I give away my power and what steps can I take to call it back?

Explore the realms of your subconscious to uncover some buried desires. This new Moon can feel intense because it's here to wake you up to your own magic. It's an invitation to call your power back from the situations that have had you under a spell and living life on auto-pilot. Don't get caught up in the blame game: start making some new rules. This is a potent time to break bad habits, heal a broken heart and connect with your life purpose.

◈ Smoky quartz
● Water
● Pluto and Mars

FULL MOON IN SCORPIO
Transformation; intimacy; relationships; obsession

Journal prompt: How can I build stronger foundations for myself?

Rise above difficult times. You may notice that your intuitive senses are heightened so you are quick to call out anyone who isn't being real with you. This full Moon can illuminate anything that's inauthentic in your life so that it can be released. What have you been clinging to? You're being called to be fearless and surrender. At times it can feel as if the universe is working against you, but these moments are the catalysts that will make you wiser and stronger. You don't have to hold it all together. Loosen your grip. Allow yourself to heal and be supported.

◈ Labradorite
● Water
● Pluto and Mars

71

SAGITTARIUS MOONCAST
Positive; adventurous; day-dreamer

You're likely to be feeling upbeat when the Moon is in Sagittarius, planning your next big adventure, looking up flights, or booking tickets for a festival during your lunch break. You may be researching your latest idea or wanting to break free, convinced there must be more to life than being stuck at a desk from nine until five. You may feel unstoppable, tempted to take a risk. There's a fine line between spontaneity and being reckless. Check your facts, responsibilities and bank balance before taking a leap of faith. You may find yourself being flirtatious: give yourself the push to go on a date.

NEW MOON IN SAGITTARIUS
Adventure; expansion; optimism; taking risks

Journal prompt: List all of the things you wish you could do but don't make time for.
Commit to doing at least one once a week.

Broaden your horizons – the world is your oyster! This new Moon can feel expansive and optimistic. You may not be able to jump on a plane to the other side of the world tomorrow but you can start making plans. Itchy feet? Find out if any cultural experiences are happening locally, explore your neighbourhood, start learning a new language, or go on a spontaneous day out. If you're feeling stuck in a rut, channel this Sagittarian energy to start exploring new interests, or learning about other philosophies to expand your mind, and get real about what's been holding you back.

◈ Fuchsite
♦ Fire
● Jupiter

FULL MOON IN SAGITTARIUS
Expansion; travel; confidence; hope

Journal prompt: What does freedom mean to me?

Get clear on what (or where) you're aiming for, just like the archer preparing to shoot their arrows. A full Moon brings culmination: as these moonbeams join forces with Sagittarius you may feel it's time to spread your wings. This lunar dose of optimism may help you take some necessary risks. Be mindful when dropping truth bombs that you aren't burning bridges: you won't know if you may need them again. There will be times where you feel you're taking one step forward and two steps back but just think of an arrow being launched: it has to be pulled backwards before it can take flight.

◈ Rutilated quartz
♦ Fire
● Jupiter

CAPRICORN MOONCAST
Motivation; persistence; drive

If there's something you've found yourself procrastinating over, you may experience a boost in motivation and focus when the Moon is in Capricorn. It's time to work out your strategies and make some big plans. This zodiac sign is tenacious and practical; it creates an ideal climate for business and professional ventures. Self-discipline may come easier when the Moon is in Capricorn. The general mood may be sober and conservative. You may also notice an undercurrent of anxiety, depression and doubt. Keep your eyes on your prize and believe in yourself.

NEW MOON IN CAPRICORN
Structure; goals; ambition; work

Journal prompt: What is it about my goals that excites me?

Time to set some goals, which all new Moons are about, but with Capricorn's tenacious influence you may find it easier to see things through to the finish. Your goals may feel like mountains you have to climb but when this zodiac sign joins forces with the new Moon, it may give you the self-discipline to stay focused. Implement some structure and strategies so that you can turn your dreams into plans. Set high standards, but check in with the ways in which you are too critical of yourself and others. Sometimes done is better than perfect.

◈ Amazonite
⛰ Earth
♄ Saturn

FULL MOON IN CAPRICORN
Authority; resilience; focus; tenacity

Journal prompt: What am I procrastinating over and why?

Reflect on the goals you set during the new Moon in Capricorn and what you've achieved in the last six months: you may be surprised by just how much has manifested if you've kept your eye on the prize. Make sure you celebrate your accomplishments. Take note of the lessons you've learnt along the way and how they've made you stronger. If you've been more procrastination than manifestation, these moonbeams may re-motivate you.

◈ Pyrite
⛰ Earth
♄ Saturn

AQUARIUS MOONCAST
Innovation; futurism; individuality

It's time to think outside the box as the Moon moves through Aquarius. We're all weirdos at heart: embrace what makes you different and use it to your advantage. Aquarius is known to be cutting-edge and visionary: you may feel an urge to rebel against political systems or at least the latest rule your boss is trying to enforce. Reality (and fact) check yourself, if you're inclined to challenge the status quo. At this time, people may seem outgoing and open to new ideas: explore alternative therapies, pioneering technology, trailblazing thought-leaders and activism. Harness this collaborative energy to make the world a better place.

NEW MOON IN AQUARIUS
Radical; visionary; clarity; cutting-edge

Journal prompt: How can I embrace what makes me unique?

Rationalize how you feel with the truth of the matter. This cosmic check-in can help you detach from your emotions and become crystal clear on what actually needs attention. Aquarius is known to be the visionary of the zodiac and its influence can inspire you to embrace what makes you unique. If you've got an idea for something that may be considered 'woo-woo' or has never been done before, trust yourself and go with it. Follow an unbeaten path, whether it's related to your career, relationships or lifestyle: your family, friends and peers may not agree but it makes total sense to you, as long as you aren't putting yourself in danger or hurting anyone.

◈ Apophyllite
◎ Air
● Uranus and Saturn

FULL MOON IN AQUARIUS
Revolution; independence; humanitarianism

Journal prompt: Write your personal mission statement.

Reflect on what is relevant to you. Circumstances change but we're often caught up in doing things on auto-pilot. Let go of what isn't working for you, use what you've learnt and innovate. Is it time for a rebrand or reboot? Aquarius is known to be the eccentric of the zodiac and it can be an idealist at heart. It's ruled by Uranus, the planet associated with awakening and sudden changes. Under this influence things may seem unpredictable and have the potential to take you down a new path that you would never have imagined. Surrender and stay open.

◈ Chrysocolla
◎ Air
● Uranus and Saturn

PISCES MOONCAST
Empathetic; introspective; romantic

Feeling feelings: this describes the Moon's energy as it moves through Pisces. Empathy can be running high during this time: be careful not to drown in other people's emotions as the lines may blur between what's yours to process and what's theirs. Boundaries are important: without them, you may feel overwhelmed and easily triggered. On the flipside, the mood can be romantic, comforting, dreamy, sleepy and artistic. Use this time to unleash your inner mystic: meditate, immerse yourself in a ritual bath, do an oracle or Tarot reading for yourself, cast spells. You may notice that your dreams are more vivid: keep a dream journal close by so that you can interpret any hidden messages from your subconscious.

NEW MOON IN PISCES
Wisdom; romance; imagination; empathy

Journal prompt: During the two days leading up to the new Moon in Pisces and the two days afterwards, keep your journal next to your bed. As soon as you wake up in the morning, write about and describe your dreams to see if there are any subliminal messages.

Turn up the volume to your intuition and cultivate a deeper connection with the world around you. These moonbeams can seem ethereal and tug at your heartstrings. You may notice that you're more emotionally sensitive, and if you need to have a cry, let the tears fall. Ask for support or a hug if you need it. Pisces' influence on the new Moon can act as a spiritual healing. Align with this lunation to pinpoint what prevents you from listening to your inner guidance. Make time for things that nourish your soul, like art, music, poetry, spirituality and mysticism. Don't hide your magic.

◈ Lapis lazuli
● Water
● Neptune

FULL MOON IN PISCES
Healing; addictions; codependency; intuition

Journal prompt: How do I avoid experiencing my feelings and how could I set some healthy boundaries to support me?

Dive into the depths of your emotions to understand what you need to release. When the full Moon joins forces with Pisces, the conjunction may feel like an emotional rollercoaster. It can turn up the volume to your psychic abilities, which may be overwhelming for some: it's tempting to block them out because you're feeling too much. During this lunation, make sure you put some boundaries in place so that you can process what's coming up for you. This is a potent time to ride the waves that can lead you to cultivate compassion and forgiveness.

◈ Howlite
● Water
● Neptune

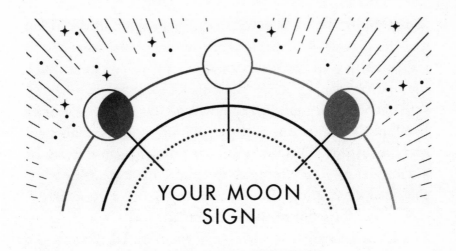

YOUR MOON
SIGN

Most people know their Sun sign (also known as star or zodiac sign) and that of their loved ones – who doesn't use astrology to try to gain a better understanding of someone they've just started dating? – but aren't aware that astrology actually relates to where *all* of the celestial bodies are positioned at our date and time of birth. That is why you may not totally relate to the description of your sign or horoscope: you are so much more than your Sun sign.

YOU ARE MORE THAN
YOUR SUN SIGN

Sun signs are the easiest to figure out because they're based on where among the twelve zodiac signs the Sun was placed when you were born, but they only offer a glimpse into something much more expansive. The position of the Moon and the planets, at the moment you were born, also has an influence on your personality and the way you move through life. Astrology is a science: there's a lot to decipher.

A deeper understanding of how it all relates to you is like a handbook that explains your personality, motives, challenges and life lessons. This knowledge is power because it can be a reminder of your strengths and also what aspects of yourself need developing. As much as we all love a good astrology meme for a flutter of validation, astrology is a dynamic tool for self-awareness and transformation. I'd recommend having an astrology reading with a professional astrologer to learn more about the intricacies of your chart and what makes you unique so that you can use the insights and guidance to your advantage.

Astrologers to follow (and get a reading from):
Francesca Oddie @francescaoddieastrology
Madeleine Botet de Lacaze @astrologyforartists
Kimberly Peta Dewhirst, founder of
Star Sign Style @starsignstyle
AstroStyle by The AstroTwins @astrotwins
Chani Nicholas @chaninicholas
Annabel Gat @annabelgat
Valerie Mesa @valeriemesa
Jaliessa Sipress @jaliessasipress

CALCULATING YOUR BIRTH CHART

To find out what all of the celestial bodies are saying about you, you'll need to have an astrology birth chart. It's a map of the sky that charts the exact positions of the Sun, Moon and planets on the zodiac wheel, according to the moment you were born. Nowadays, an astrology app is only ever a few thumb taps away on a screen, or google 'astrology birth chart', but if you want a more in-depth reading, I'd recommend booking in with an astrologer.

For your birth chart, you'll need to input your date of birth, where you were born and, for the most accurate reading, your time of birth. If you've got forgetful parents (like mine) and you can't determine the exact time, you can still check out your birth chart but you won't get an accurate reading for your rising sign or which houses the planets fall in. You'll still gain insight, though, from entering your date and location of birth, like your natal Moon sign.

UNDERSTANDING YOUR MOON SIGN

It is important to know your Moon sign because a little bit of emotional intelligence can go a long way. The first time I tuned into what my Moon sign was telling me, my mind was blown. Have you seen those penny machines at seaside amusement arcades? You keep putting in coins through a slot until one lands in the sweet spot and a load of pennies cascade over the edge. Jackpot! Well, that was how I felt after spending some time with my Moon sign. At the time, my boyfriend and I were going through a rocky patch and our Moon signs helped me to understand what was going on with us. My Moon is in Aquarius and his is in Taurus, which helped to illustrate how different our emotional needs are and why we were clashing so much at the time. It's up to us to go on a journey through self-discovery to be able to understand our own needs so that we can communicate them to others. Think of sex: how can you expect your lover to know how to turn you on if you don't totally know?

Understanding your Moon sign can illuminate what you need to feel safe and rooted, even when life gets crazy. It helps you to understand what feeds you on an emotional level. When you experience stress, trauma, heartbreak or conflict, your Moon sign will come into play and you will subconsciously react according to what it is drawn to for security. I always think of the Moon sign as the side of you that people only get to know when you trust them, or when you're on holiday, away from your usual safety net. There will be times when you try to override your needs for others and forget about yourself. Come back to your Moon sign to help you find your way home.

NATAL MOON IN ARIES

Loves: Freedom and independence to do whatever you want

Triggers: Not being the one in charge and frustrated when things aren't going as quickly as you'd like

Nourishment: Spontaneity, excitement and taking risks

De-stress: Move your body to burn off excess energy; dancing, cardiovascular exercise or sex/self-pleasure

NATAL MOON IN TAURUS

Loves: Stability, security and creature comforts

Triggers: Any kind of financial uncertainty and unexpected change

Nourishment: Spending time with family and loved ones, and being able to do things at your own pace

De-stress: Get your nature fix outdoors or treat yourself to a massage to ease the tension that's built up in your neck and shoulders

NATAL MOON IN GEMINI

Loves: Learning new things and being sociable; networking is second nature to you

Triggers: Getting the silent treatment and lack of dialogue

Nourishment: Channelling all of your ideas and having somewhere (or someone) to share them with. This doesn't mean you have to act on all of them!

De-stress: Pick up the phone and call your best friend, if you need a sounding board. Alternatively, get your journal and write your heart out. Need to go deeper? Book a session with a therapist to help you process your emotions, instead of over-analyzing

NATAL MOON IN CANCER

Loves: Retreating from the world into hygge (Danish word, meaning ultra cosiness and well-being)

Triggers: Feeling unappreciated and abandoned

Nourishment: Healthy boundaries: it's safe to say no. JOMO (joy of missing out) is your friend

De-stress: You may have a tendency to feel intensely: Cancer is ruled by the Moon. Find an outlet to channel your deep emotions, perhaps through a creative pursuit where you can turn what you're feeling into art, or talk to a therapist so that you can offload and process in a safe, non-biased space

NATAL MOON IN LEO

Loves: Being the centre of attention and would give anything for an easy life

Triggers: Feeling bored, ignored and undervalued

Nourishment: Follow your passions: a sense of achievement is important to you

De-stress: Wear something that makes you feel the bomb; leave your hair loose and wild; go out and dance to blow some cobwebs away

NATAL MOON IN VIRGO

Loves: Solving problems, creating systems and perfecting things

Triggers: Disorganization and anything that puts your health and well-being at risk

Nourishment: Making plans and sorting out your home/ workspace

De-stress: Make sure that you schedule regular time for yourself and make it non-negotiable: if it's scheduled it's more likely to happen. Prevention is better than burnout. Don't feel guilty about cancelling plans with other people if it benefits your mental health

NATAL MOON IN LIBRA

Loves: Falling in love, being in love and spreading the love

Triggers: Any kind of conflict or feeling out of balance

Nourishment: Being in peaceful and inspiring environments helps you relax . . .

De-stress: Practising yoga can help you get out of your thoughts and into your body, also working on your balance!

NATAL MOON IN SCORPIO

Loves: Conflict, intensity and passion

Triggers: Life feels too settled and calm

Nourishment: Nurturing relationships with people you trust. Learning to trust is a big thing for you but oh-so-worthwhile when you find the good ones

De-stress: Long baths, and listening to music that reflects how you're feeling: let the tears fall if you need to cry

NATAL MOON IN SAGITTARIUS

Loves: Adventure, hedonism and new experiences

Triggers: Losing your passport and any situation in which you feel your wings have been clipped

Nourishment: Meeting new people and exploring new places and cultures

De-stress: If you're feeling stuck, practise gratitude and focus on the things you can do. You might find a clue in your list that can make you feel free again

NATAL MOON IN CAPRICORN

Loves: Goals, goals, goals

Triggers: Losing the spark for your ambitions

Nourishment: Achieving your goals. Don't forget to enjoy the journey

De-stress: Spend some time on your own to reset and recharge: a break could give you the space to realize a strategy that makes your life easier and gets your head back in the game

NATAL MOON IN AQUARIUS

Loves: Friends, collaboration and being a rebel with a cause

Triggers: Commitment can freak you out; feeling trapped or overcrowded – you need your space

Nourishment: Daring to be different

De-stress: Be spontaneous and break any self-imposed rules. Spending time among people you can fly your freak flag with can be so liberating

NATAL MOON IN PISCES

Loves: All things mystical and expressing your soul through creativity

Triggers: Feeling as if you're losing yourself in other people's emotions and chaos

Nourishment: Making sure that the people you spend time with and home/work environments are in sync with you

De-stress: It can be overwhelming being so empathic: cut the cords of codependent relationships or at least enforce some much-needed boundaries so you have the space to process your own feelings

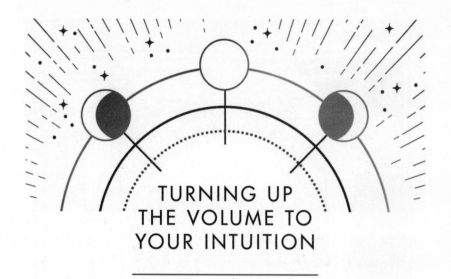

TURNING UP
THE VOLUME TO
YOUR INTUITION

The Moon is associated with our instinct, feelings, magnetism, subconscious, receptivity, reflection, dreams, femininity and intuition; it guides us to understand our inner truths and embody them. This energy is represented by the High Priestess in the Tarot: she's devoted to aligning with higher states of consciousness and knowing herself. She utilizes intuition over intellect. She is still. The High Priestess has nothing to prove. Self-trust is her superpower. You could think of her as the cover girl for the Moon. Becoming more like the High Priestess can't happen overnight: it's a journey of building trust. She's an archetypal energy that's within you. You could think of it as getting to know your woke BFF to the point that you're finishing their sentences. Have you seen those memes that depict what we think spiritual awakening should look like versus the reality of it? You may think it's

The high priestess

about being all love and light, 24/7, but the truth is you will be tested at times as you navigate the new terrain. That's how we really learn and integrate new levels of awareness. This isn't meant to scare you off: you've got this.

Aligning with the Moon can support you to turn up the volume to your intuition, whether through practising rituals or increased emotional intelligence. As you become more self-aware, understanding your moods, triggers and fluctuating energy levels throughout the cycle, you can slow down and find your own rhythm: you're able to discern whether it's your truth you're experiencing or someone else's. The lines may blur when you're stressed and anxious.

Intuition isn't reserved for a lucky few. We are all intuitive, *even* the natural-born over-thinkers, the practical ones and the sceptics. Even if you don't identify as intuitive, I know you can call out inauthenticity when you see it. You may know it as a gut instinct, inner voice or sixth sense. Intuition is innate, regardless of your upbringing, religion, gender or experience. But it isn't always the loudest voice in your head, which is why it's often dismissed. The conscious mind processes information based on what we 'think', which is often based on previous experiences or external influences. Intuition is more sensitive to subtleties that may otherwise go under the radar. That is why you may associate your intuition with feeling, rather than thinking. Most of us aren't taught how to translate the messages that our intuition tries to send us so we play it safe: the message is sent to voicemail to be picked up later, often with a twinge of regret – we wish we'd listened to it sooner.

Intuition is an awareness of a situation or a prompt that's instinctive: you just know something (which isn't based on previous experience) or get a nudge to do something that seems out of the blue, or a niggle that won't go away. It can be a sense of clarity, beyond any logic or prior information to back it up. Like hearing your phone ring and instantly you know that the friend you were just thinking about is calling, or that someone's not going to turn up for an appointment, or when a friend introduces you to their latest lover, there's a feeling in your gut that there's something shady about him or her. And there's that moment when you're house-hunting and you know you've found your new home, or you take a different route because you suddenly feel like it and bump into a friend who hooks you up with an incredible opportunity.

'I don't know how I know, I just do' usually accompanies an intuitive nudge.

When it comes to your intuition, first impressions count: the gut feeling or hunch – whether it's about an opportunity, person, house, job or relationship – is trying to tell you something. The trick is not to talk yourself out of it.

Decisions are often made based on what you think you *should* do, despite the glaring red flags, or reasoning based on circumstances and outcomes from the past, or obligations and people-pleasing (one of the surest ways to put your intuition on flight mode). Your intuition doesn't conform to any of these, which may make it hard to trust: there isn't any evidence, yet, to back it up.

If you're over-thinking a decision, it's probably because there's a conflict between what your intuition is guiding you towards and what you think you *should* do. It wants to lead you towards the truth, which may be hidden beneath obligations, fears and vulnerability. It's there to guide us towards a higher purpose, rather than letting us get caught up in all of the outdated details and drama. Your intuition won't always tell you what you want to hear and it can take you out of your comfort zone: feeling the push and pull of resistance is part of the process.

Intuition is a tenacious force: it won't take it personally if you ignore it. It will be there in the background (sometimes nagging), even if someone is trying to gaslight you, until you honour it or the situation runs its course and you realize it was right all along.

There's nothing more frustrating than knowing you could have followed a different path when you convinced yourself otherwise: you get angry with the world around you and it's someone else's fault for leading you astray. At the end of the day, though, you've got to own your decisions and take responsibility. View it as an opportunity to give your intuition a high-five for being wiser than you realized at the time – and remember: listen up, next time.

If you're repeating the same pattern again and again, but getting the same (undesired or outworn) results, what if you tried something different? What if you follow your intuition to see where it takes you? As humans, we can get stuck in our ways, and trick ourselves into thinking it's better the devil you know. But what if your intuition was leading you in an ultimately better direction?

Being intuitive isn't about always making the 'right' choice and living a life of divine ease: a mistake can teach us a much-needed lesson that we won't forget.

Sometimes you have to make a few 'wrong' moves to wise up.

You don't need to go into the depths of a jungle and take part in a sacred ayahuasca ceremony to awaken your third eye (the chakra commonly associated with intuition and heightened perception); you just need to start listening. And by listening, I don't necessarily mean with your ears, although some of you may receive some of your intuitive downloads, nudges and pings in that way. Listening to your intuition can mean tuning into the sensations in your body when you need to make a decision, how your energy shifts when you're with someone or when an idea comes to you in the shower.

You already use your intuition daily when you're interacting with others: it may come as a first impression of someone you've just met, or you know something's wrong even though your friend is trying to convince you otherwise. If you work in a public-facing role, like a hairdresser, therapist, waiter, customer-service adviser, personal assistant or consultant, you're tuning into other people to work out how you can be of best service to them. If you're a parent you may sense what your child needs without them physically or verbally communicating it. It can be as if you're reading someone's mind or between the lines in what they say. It's like we have access to another channel and we can receive what's known as downloads. It may be an idea that comes out of the blue: perhaps it's taking your umbrella to work even though the sun is shining; or picking up an item from a shop for a friend – when you give it to them, they tell you that they'd lost theirs (how did you know?) – or a nudge to call a friend you haven't spoken to for a while and they tell you they dreamt of you last night. Your intuition can speak to you in your dreams, giving you information or what can seem to be a premonition. It picks up on things that your conscious mind doesn't notice. Intuition isn't analytical: it doesn't weigh up the pros and cons, or even consider the facts, which is why it's often disregarded.

Your intuition is your highest intelligence because it isn't caught up in people-pleasing or seeking external validation. It isn't about being right or wrong: it's there to guide you towards higher ground.

You could think of your intuition as a muscle you can strengthen or a relationship in which you're building trust. Get to know it. Lean into it.

When you get an intuitive nudge, take note of how it feels and how it's communicated to you. Look out for the nuances. What's happening when you get a download? You may notice it has a different tone compared to your usual thoughts. It can seem like a lightning bolt out of nowhere or a penny finally dropping. Sometimes it's hushed but crystal clear. Perhaps it happens when you're in the shower or brushing your teeth or chopping vegetables for a stir-fry. It's likely that you'll find your intuition is clearer and louder when you're meditating or relaxed enough for your brain to shift into a theta state (just before and just after sleeping), during a Moon ceremony or ritual, a Tarot reading, or simply somewhere quiet in nature. Those precious moments when you aren't distracted by the world around you. Completely in the present.

Try not to cherry-pick what your intuition's telling you.

Of course it's easier to listen and take action when it's saying something nice and easy, like choosing a crystal or you pull an oracle card and it gives you a positive reading, but when it comes to doing something beyond your comfort zone or it's telling you something you don't want to hear, you tend to dismiss it, thinking that the signal has dropped and its message has been lost in translation.

Your intuition can be subtle but is communicated through psychic senses, known as the 'clairs' (meaning clear in French).

THE SIX PSYCHIC SENSES

Clairvoyance. This is the 'clair' you're most likely to have heard of. It means 'clear seeing'. With this psychic sense you'll see visions: it can be very similar to dreams. They may appear to you when you're in a meditative or light sleep state. You may be aware of colours in and around your body, or it's as if you're watching a screen and something's being acted out, or you see symbols, scenery, objects, written words, animals, spirit guides, angels and people. Clairvoyance is also associated with lucid dreaming, in which you can consciously interact with your dreamscape. This psychic sense may freak some people out: what if you see something you don't want to see, like a ghost or something that could be perceived as bad? While this happens for some, I think it's quite rare because fear overrides it so those things can't come through.

Clairsentience. This is about 'clear feeling': when you notice

physical sensations in your body. It can simply be the awareness of how your body reacts to certain people or situations.
Clairsentience may cause you to feel someone else's pain,
whether it's physical or emotional; you may feel the pain as
a sudden backache or heaviness. Picking up on another person's well-being is also possible but is often subtler. I know
this is going to sound creepy but in some cases it can literally
be as if you sense someone is touching you or something's
brushed past you. It may be one of your spirit guides.

Clairaudience. This means 'clear hearing' and most commonly occurs when you're doing a guided meditation or journey
and you're given an opportunity to ask questions in a conversation with a spirit guide or with your higher self. You may
receive an answer from another voice speaking internally (in
your mind). You may also hear music, lyrics, sounds or words
that are coming from within. Sometimes a voice comes out
of nowhere with a message.

Claircognizance. The ability to know something without learning or being told about it, which can make it tricky to back
up. You may sense that a friend is unexpectedly pregnant,
or know where a lost object will be in a house you've never
been to before, or suddenly decide to catch an earlier train
and find out later that there was an accident on the one after
yours, or in a guided meditation you access information you
had no prior knowledge of. A claircognizant friend intuits
unusual names that seem random, but when she researches
their meaning they're so relevant to her situation.

Clairalience. This means 'clear smell': in certain situations, such as when you're in a meditative state or just about to go to sleep, a scent wafts under your nose. It may be familiar: flowers that remind you of a loved one, or a perfume, or even the smell of a specific brand of cigarette.

Clairgustance. 'Clear taste': in a similar way to clairalience, you get a taste in your mouth of something distinctive. I had a friend who went to see a psychic, who asked, 'Who's close to you who likes Jaffa Cakes? I can taste them and it's horrible.' The psychic clearly wasn't a lover of Jaffa Cakes but my friend immediately knew who it related to.

It can be tricky trying to determine if it's your intuition or anxiety speaking. It's like when you're in the car and you've got lost because you're driving too fast and missed the turning you needed to take. When you're feeling anxious, your energy system is overloaded and your thoughts are scattered. Being in an alpha brain state, where you're calm, quiet and somewhere you aren't distracted, can support you to tune into these senses and get to know which of them your intuition communicates through. You may be in a light sleep state, dreaming, meditating, doing creative visualization, writing, daydreaming and connecting with the subconscious. This can help you to enhance sensitivity, make sense of it all and hone your response towards the intuitive messages you're receiving. Don't rush or put pressure on yourself. It might take practice but the more you slow down, the better you can turn up the volume to your intuition.

One of the easiest ways to recognize your intuition is to rewind through all of the times that you *ignored* it: the ex you stayed with for too long; the job that had all the perks but something was saying you were selling your soul; or the investment that really was too good to be true; or the time you didn't speak up and now wish you had. How did your body feel when you were bypassing the red flags and signs? What were you consciously thinking? What was the motive behind your decision-making process? How did you talk yourself out of following your gut instinct? Were you tripped up by the 'shoulds', people-pleasing, thinking it was the logical thing to do, or you just wanted an easy life?

MEET YOUR EGO

Just like intuition, we all have an ego. It isn't as evil as people make it out to be. Your ego does whatever it can to keep you safe within the confines of your comfort zone. The ego can also represent your self-esteem and self-worth. It wants to protect you from reliving past traumas, looking a fool or feeling guilty, and it loves to dance with your limiting beliefs. Thoughts like, 'Who do you think you are? You can't do this. You will fail. What if you humiliate yourself? You don't deserve this.' These words that echo through your mind: this is your ego talking, keeping you stuck in a rut. Living your best life usually means stepping out of your comfort zone. Our ego is nuanced. I think it represents our shadow self: the parts of ourselves we're ashamed of, whatever makes us feel vulnerable and triggered. We play down our achievements because we don't want people to think we're big-headed; we shrink ourselves so that others don't think we're too much or feel threatened by us. If someone's having a bad day we can feel guilty that some incredible things are happening for us so we play down the good stuff. We just want to fit in because that's where we think we're safe. Ego can cause us to do things for external validation rather than because we want to do them. The mind is a powerful tool but a terrible master, and I think the same applies with the ego. It's good to want better for ourselves but it's important to check in with *why*.

MEET YOUR HIGHEST SELF

Your highest self is the intelligence that diminishes the put-downs your ego may use against you. It's an expanded way of thinking and being. In comparison to the ego, it's uncomplicated and unadulterated. Your highest self can also be the spokesperson for your intuition. It's your cheerleader and speaks to you in the same compassionate and encouraging way that you do with your best friends.

EGO: What if it doesn't work out?
HIGHEST SELF: What if it does?

EGO: People will judge me.
HIGHEST SELF: No one will judge you as much as you're judging yourself, right now.

EGO: Life is hard.
HIGHEST SELF: Let yourself be supported, then.

EGO: I'm not good enough yet.
HIGHEST SELF: You've got to start somewhere (and, yes, you are!).

EGO: It's too good to be true. They're going to find out that I'm a terrible person and it will be the end.
HIGHEST SELF: This is just F-E-A-R, or False Events Appearing Real. You deserve this. Enjoy it.

EGO: What if they don't like me?
HIGHEST SELF: If that's the case, they aren't your people. Just be yourself and you'll find out the truth.

EGO: If I don't do it, then who will?
HIGHEST SELF: The world will keep spinning, even if you take a day off. It's safe to say no.

Living intuitively is about trusting yourself above anyone else: nobody knows you as well as you know yourself. It's your life to live. I think that's where true confidence comes from: wholeheartedly trusting the decisions you make and proceeding accordingly. Instead of obsessively reading your horoscopes, having psychic readings to confirm that you're doing the right thing, or constantly asking your friends for advice, tune into what you want from a situation. We can give away so much of our power by letting other people make our decisions for us. Perhaps you pretend that you're the easy-going one, but the truth is that making a decision gives you anxiety because you over-think everything. It can feel safer to let someone else take the reins, but at the end of the day, the only person who will *always* be there is *you*. Why not invest in *numero uno* and speak up for what you want? Honouring your needs and desires is important.

The hold-back is that we don't trust our intuition enough because we want proof, and if our ego is leading us in a different direction, it has proof: 'Do you remember the last time you did that and it didn't work out?' or 'So-and-so did it and it worked for them' or 'If you go for this job you'll have more security and know that your bills will be covered and the holiday allowance is great, too. All you need do is sign on the dotted line . . .'

Living intuitively is based on what feels right for you, rather than what society (or your ego) may tell you. It's knowing what your truth feels like. Your intuition helps you to discern it.

HOW TO TELL IF YOUR INTUITION IS TELLING YOU YES OR NO

- Get comfortable in a place where you won't be disturbed.
- Sit down with your back straight and supported, either cross-legged or on a chair with both feet firmly on the floor.
- Rest your hands on your thighs, your palms facing up.
- Close your eyes and take three slow, deep breaths in and out.
- Scan your body and bring your attention to any areas that feel tense and breathe into that space; as you exhale feel yourself relax even more.

- Think of a situation that needs a decision.
- Imagine you are at a fork in the road: two different paths lead to alternative outcomes.
- Do you feel drawn more to the path on the left or the right? Tune into where the answer comes from. Do you feel a physical pull or other sensations in your body, or do you sense the answer in another way?
- Ask yourself why you are drawn to this path. Then ask: what is the potential outcome if you choose this one?
- Bring your attention to the other path. Ask yourself why you aren't as drawn to this path. Then ask: what is the potential outcome if you choose this one?
- Which paths represent your yes and no?
- The true answer should feel as if it lights you up, even if it seems a bit daunting. There may be a sense of apprehension or nervousness around what your intuition is telling you but you can always check in and ask yourself if you're feeling this way because it's the wrong thing to do or just because it's out of your comfort zone.

If my intuition is telling me no, I either don't notice any sensations or feel as if I'm standing in front of a closed door. I may feel heavy and as if my head is fogged. If it's a yes, I feel lighter and expansive. I feel activated and uncomplicated. This may not be the same for you. Use this visualization to get to know what your yes or no is like for you.

As I said, everyone is intuitive but the key to the good stuff? You've gotta trust it and act accordingly.

Full Moons bring illumination and can heighten your

awareness. Because the full Moon is amplifying, it may seem to turn up the volume to your intuition; it may also put lots of other things in your life under the spotlight so it's helpful to take time out to process anything that comes up for you. Meditate, journal, perhaps pull a Tarot card (or a few) to see what it's really trying to tell you. You may notice points in the Moon cycle when your dreams are more vivid. Write them down as soon as you wake up to see if there are any messages or premonitions from your intuition. Dark or new Moons can support a clear channel to your intuition because energetically it's a quieter time and easier to tune in, with potentially fewer distractions compared to the full Moon. That being said, your intuition is always there. You can't switch it on and off. You may notice that it communicates with you to varying degrees, depending on the lunation or what's going on in your life.

Your intuitive senses can be heightened and developed through practices like meditation, yoga, Tarot reading, working with crystals and breathwork (a conscious breathing practice). After they've been attuned with reiki, people often feel that they are more psychic and intuitive and are able to receive information they wouldn't have been aware of or had access to otherwise. Anyone can develop and nurture these senses.

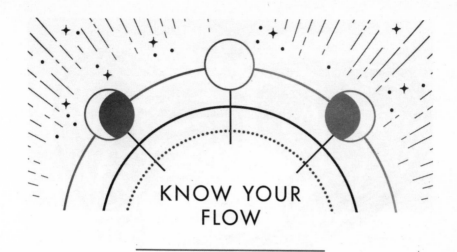

KNOW YOUR FLOW

If you're being called to connect with the Moon and your intuition, you will also need to connect with your body and attune to your own rhythms. We are cyclical beings: our bodies are innately aligned with nature and the seasons, but for some of us these cycles are more apparent. It's no coincidence that a woman's menstrual cycle is on average twenty-eight days (unless her cycles are inhibited by contraception or other reasons) and that some women are in sync with the Moon.

The menstrual cycle is part of the feminine flow. You don't have to have periods to be feminine but a monthly bleed is an obvious indicator of your inner cycle. Even if you have irregular periods or none at all, getting to know your body's rhythms can be a game changer.

In the same way that the Moon waxes and wanes, so do aspects of our body's rhythm. The first part of the menstrual

cycle is more yang as our energy builds and we may feel more outgoing, while the second is more yin as our need to rest increases and we may feel more reclusive. According to Alexandra Pope and Sjanie Hugo Wurlitzer, who have both written about menstruation, if you push yourself too much during the first part of your menstrual cycle, because you feel supercharged, there's a chance that you may experience more pain and increased PMS during the premenstrual phase.

Each phase of the menstrual cycle reflects the lunar cycle: menstruation is (energetically) similar to the dark and new Moon phases; pre-ovulation is akin to the waxing Moon, ovulation to the full Moon and premenstruation to the waning Moon. I've indicated overleaf each phase, with the corresponding Moon phase, to help you understand the characteristics, how they mirror each other and the themes you may expect.

Most of us are out of sync with our bodies and cycles: it's a common side effect of modern life. Artificial lighting disrupts our circadian rhythms; contraceptive pills and other medications override our body's natural processes; we force ourselves to go to work even when we're ill, denying ourselves time to fully recover and heal; an afternoon caffeine fix or energy drink pushes us on when we're exhausted.

Your menstrual cycle may not be in sync with the Moon cycle in timings. For example, a new Moon can be an introspective time, but if you're in the ovulation phase of your cycle, you may actually feel energized and want to put yourself out there. Or despite the full Moon's supposed celebratory mood, you may be premenstrual and navigating a dark/new Moon phase internally. It may feel conflicting if the Moon is saying one thing but your body is saying something else. You do you. First and foremost, listen to your body and how you are feeling.

Our bodies are trying to communicate with us all of the time, whether through fluctuating energy levels, illness or pain.

I find it so reassuring knowing that it's natural to fluctuate in the way we feel throughout the Moon and menstrual cycle. It's even more empowering to know we can use this information to support ourselves and potentially avoid burnout. Each phase of your cycle has its own benefits and difficulties: getting to know it can make it easier to navigate. You'll have a better understanding of what you need and can implement any adjustments in your personal or work life to make the ride smoother.

Below you'll find a Moon phase alongside each menstrual phase: this relates to the characteristics of each. Your (inner Moon) cycle might not synchronize with the Moon cycle that's happening in the sky but it will give you an idea of how you could be feeling physically and an understanding of how the phases are similar energetically.

MENSTRUATION

This is the beginning of the menstrual cycle; the day that you start bleeding is the first day of your cycle. During this phase your body may be calling you to rest and make self-care more of a priority.

Moon Phase: Dark/new Moon

Season: Winter

Mood: Wise, perceptive, feeling overwhelmed and introverted

Themes: Low energy, rest, release, self-care and boundaries

PRE-OVULATION

This is the first phase of the cycle, which comes after you've finished bleeding. It can feel as if a fog has lifted and you can expect a gradual upswing in your energy with a renewed sense of enthusiasm for life.

Moon Phase: Waxing Moon

Season: Spring

Mood: Enthusiastic, optimistic, easy-going, daring and creative

Themes: Getting things done, starting projects, taking a leap and socializing

OVULATION

This is the second phase of the cycle, when you're most fertile: one of your ovaries is due to release an egg. During this phase your hormones can feel as if they're on your side; you may notice a surge in confidence.

Moon Phase: Full Moon

Season: Summer

Mood: Sensual, creative, fertile, aligned and empowered

Themes: Feeling confident, magnetic, nurturing, procreative and making things happen

PREMENSTRUAL

This is the last phase of your cycle. After you've ovulated you may notice a shift in your mood and behaviour. Don't give yourself a hard time: honour what you need.

Moon Phase: Waning Moon

Season: Autumn

Mood: Emotional, sensitive, irritable, depressed and anxious

Themes: Intuitive, efficient, truth-telling and problem-solving

---

Be mindful of what the Moon is saying but, most importantly, tune into what your body is telling you and observe how you're feeling. Some may say you're likely to feel a certain way according to the Moon phase or your menstrual cycle but that doesn't mean it's true for you. If you have periods, your cycle may not be in sync with the timings of the Moon or correspond with how you feel during your menstrual cycle. Tune into what's true for you and what you need in every moment, regardless of the Moon phase.

GETTING TO KNOW YOUR CYCLE

Each day, track your energy levels, moods, emotions, appetite, sex drive, mental state and sleep.

Lots of apps are designed specifically to monitor your wellbeing. I use a period and cycle tracker app. I like to use Clue because it's simple to use and I can add information throughout my cycle; it has different categories and options that I can log, if applicable, predicts when I'll ovulate and when my period is due. I often refer to this information when I'm planning things. Alternatively, you could simply input some emojis on your phone calendar or add these details to your journal at the end of each day.

If you have periods, I'd recommend starting on day one (the first day of your bleed) of your menstrual cycle. For those who don't have periods, you could start tracking on a new Moon or the first day of the month. In fact, you can start tracking any time you want to. Commit to doing this for at least three months, but don't worry if you miss a day here and there. As soon as you remember, log in something. You could set a daily reminder to help you get into a routine with it. Over time you're likely to find patterns emerging if you're consistent.

When you track, you can start to see what is and isn't working for you. You're able to monitor your health and potentially detect early anything that may be of concern. For example, when life gets busy, it can be easy to lose track of time and not realize that your periods have been irregular for a year; you may want to consult a doctor. It may also help you get the right treatment sooner if you've got evidence to back you up.

HOW CAN I SYNC
WITH MY CYCLE?

After you've been tracking for a while you may notice that you have 'good' and 'bad' days at specific times of your cycle. For example, on the days preceding my period I usually feel tired, I get abdominal cramps and my head seems fogged, which isn't ideal when I need to write to a deadline. I used to try to push through because I 'needed' to get things done, but no matter how hard I tried to be productive it was as if I was walking through mud and nothing flowed. My inner critic would have a field day. When I realized the pattern, I saw that it was pointless forcing things when I'd inevitably have to do the same work again on an easier day of my cycle. This has given me the confidence to surrender to my symptoms and take things easy when I'm premenstrual/menstruating.

Utilize your optimal days and be more forgiving when you aren't feeling your best. Get to know which days you're most likely to feel like a super-hero and make plans to do things that may require you to be more extroverted or to multi-task.

Get to know the days when you're easily triggered and irritated, and make sure your schedule allows you to do things that keep you feeling calmer. Get to know when your existential crisis days are so you can ride the wave and avoid doing anything impulsive you may regret later. Hopefully, this will help you to realize you aren't crazy or failing at life, just experiencing all of the facets of being a human and that we're constantly transitioning from one phase to the next.

When you start to live in alignment with your cycle, you're less likely to experience stress, burnout and feeling overwhelmed because it takes more energy to swim against the current.

To learn more about the menstrual cycle, I recommend reading Maisie Hill's *Period Power*, Lisa Lister's *Code Red*, Alexandra Pope and Sjanie Hugo Wurlitzer's *Wild Power*, and Alisa Vitti's *WomanCode*.

HELL, YEAH, SELF-CARE

Don't you just wish you could keep those holiday/retreat/deep meditation/healing session feelings flowing? You can. It's called self-care. There's a common misconception that self-care involves lavish baths, retail 'therapy', eating ice cream and buying yourself flowers. It actually involves boundaries around your time and energy, feeling confident to say no, calling in sick when you're ill, getting a good night's sleep, choosing not to take criticism from someone you'd never go to for advice, walking away from toxic relationships, and making time for the things that recharge your batteries and allow you to keep evolving.

Self-care shouldn't be reserved as a reward or remedy for burnout; prevention is better than cure. A little bit of time for yourself every day or at least a few times a week can go a long way. You could try developing a meditation practice, going to a yoga session once a week, walking in nature, spending time with the people who make you smile so much that your cheeks ache, taking a break from social media at the weekends or giving yourself a digital curfew so that your inbox or notifications aren't the first and last things you see every day, having date nights or taking yourself on a date, orgasms, scheduling in time for your interests and honouring exactly where you are in every moment.

It seems counter-intuitive to take time out to catch your breath when a million and one things demand your attention, but when you do time expands. When you zoom out, you can see things from a fresh perspective and, rather than doing things the long way around, you'll most likely discover creative solutions that you'd never have considered otherwise. It's one of the reasons why I prioritize meditation and journalling: if I dive straight into the day without checking in with myself, I often miss clues as to how I can make my life easier. When you practise self-care regularly, you can cultivate new coping mechanisms for when life throws you a wild card.

There are times during the lunar cycle when it's as if you're riding an emotional rollercoaster. We're here to feel it all, even when we don't want to. The Moon invites us to embrace the ebb and flow of life because they're part of the process. Knowing this may help us to understand that we don't need to have all of the answers all of the time. Hello, dark Moon!

Sometimes self-care is just asking yourself what you truly need, when you're having a meltdown because you aren't going to make a deadline at work or you're crying in the shower because you've just found out that your ex is in a new relationship. Close your eyes, take a deep breath in for the count of six and exhale for the count of seven. Place your hand over your heart and ask yourself: what will support me today? Perhaps you get a nudge to cancel your plans that evening, to make a cup of tea, to call a friend or unfollow someone on social media. Perhaps it's a reminder to take things one step at a time and to breathe. Honour the message that comes up for you. Don't wait for life to feel as if it's been turned upside down before you do this. Try it now. Close your eyes and get curious: what will support you today? You could do this at the beginning of each day: it's a simple, yet beautiful, ritual to rise above the stresses of everyday life and connect with your highest self. This could be one of your acts of self-care.

• • • FIVE WAYS TO PRACTISE SELF-CARE • • •
(Without Spending Any Money)

1. The Magic Word
People-pleaser, I see you: anxious, overwhelmed, feeling trapped and on the edge of a meltdown because you're spinning too many plates. I want you to take a moment to do a little audit. How many yeses are you saying to others regardless of your own needs? If the result is a landslide that's definitely not in your favour, it's time to start flexing a word that begins with N and ends with O. Rather than putting yourself to the back of the queue, put yourself first for a change.

2. JOMO (joy of missing out)
We're all familiar with this feeling: you go out despite every cell in your body telling you it would be better to stay in. Fast forward to later on, and you're in a taxi wondering why you bothered. If you aren't in the mood, have neither the money nor the time, don't force yourself to do something you don't want to do. Reschedule or suggest doing something that suits everyone, yourself included.

3. Pause

Before you reply to a message or email that's triggered you, take a step back before you start typing. Make sure you haven't misinterpreted what's been said because you're in a rush, or that you aren't projecting past experiences onto what's happening right now. Check yourself before you wreck yourself. There's nothing worse than reading a message a second time and realizing you'd taken it the wrong way.

4. Ask

. . . for help. Anxiety can be a sign that you're overloaded. Perhaps something's happening in your life that you need time to process but you keep trying to push through anyway, or you've taken on too much and don't know how you'll get it all done. If you're feeling swamped, you don't have to do this alone. Take some things off your to-do list, delegate or reach out to someone who can lend a hand. Don't over-commit yourself or feel you have to respond to people immediately. Ask if you can get back to them tomorrow/next week/next month so that you've space to manoeuvre.

5. Compassion

Compassion is a two-way street; we often think it's something we direct to those around us, but self-compassion can be a radical act of self-care. Consider how you'd react if you heard someone speak to one of your loved ones in the way you speak negatively to yourself. If you keep putting yourself down for your mistakes and 'flaws', how can you believe you deserve better?

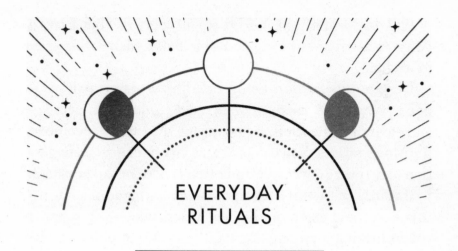

EVERYDAY RITUALS

Weaving rituals into your daily life can help you nurture your relationship with yourself and cultivate more self-awareness and emotional intelligence. Using them as check-ins can help you to process anything that's coming up for you or insights that have come through from doing the Moon rituals (see page 213). When you step away from mundane tasks to tune in with a ritual, you may shift your perspective and potentially realize creative solutions to problems. Many times, while performing a ritual, I've had ideas that have made my life easier. Ideas I would never have had if I'd dived straight into my day without meditating or journalling. I don't know about you but I'd rather move through my day with a clear intention (with which all of these everyday rituals can support you), rather than chasing my tail and feeling as if my day's a minefield. That was how I used to feel before I made these rituals non-negotiable.

Full disclosure: I don't do them all every day but I try to do them as often as I can because it makes such a difference to my life.

Despite this section being titled 'everyday rituals', you don't have to do them all every day, unless you want to and have the time for it. It just means they aren't specific to the Moon phases. You can pick and mix or choose a suggestion to do every day. Little and often is better than not at all.

If you'd like to start a regular practice with one or a few rituals, you could begin on the new Moon, which will support you in making it an ongoing habit: this Moon phase can be beneficial for starting new regimens. For the procrastinators among us: don't wait until the next new Moon. *Carpe diem.* Any time is a good time to start.

MEDITATION:
HEAVILY MEDITATED

I found meditation almost accidentally when I was trying different practices to support me in overcoming my anxiety. I went to my first yoga class at the local sports centre and, although I moved clumsily through the positions (asanas), I was really good at the savasana, the bit at the end where you lie down. I could feel myself really getting into the guided meditation, and I thought, 'Maybe meditation isn't just for super-spiritual types after all.'

Back then, I didn't know anyone who meditated. These days, we're spoilt for choice with apps that offer a plethora of

• • • BENEFITS OF MEDITATION • • •

- Creativity
- Clarity
- Mood stability
- Anger management
- Resilience to stress and challenges
- Improved sleep
- Reduced pain
- Improved memory and focus
- Motivation
- Reduced anxiety, stress, panic attacks, symptoms of stress-related conditions, such as post-traumatic stress, irritable bowel syndrome and fibromyalgia

meditation practices to choose from. Your favourite teachers most probably have recordings available to download, while meditation-appropriate music can be found on Spotify – and then there's YouTube. A lot of it's free. And you can meditate almost anywhere, as long as you won't be disturbed. Meditation couldn't be easier, in theory anyway.

In reality, it can be a struggle to slow down your thoughts when you've got a million and one things waiting for you on the other side of whatever guided meditation you might be listening to on your phone.

No matter how good we know something is for us, it's normal to fall off the wagon every now and again. It's part of the process. It's part of the meditation: the awareness to come back to yourself. When you're in meditation and your thoughts wander to something like an online order that needs returning or a conversation that's been playing on your mind (save all of that for your journalling, page 131) or whether you're doing it right, just return your focus to your breathing and listen to the music or words that are being spoken by your meditation guide.

Remember: meditation is called a practice for a reason. Let's be real: who can entirely switch off their thoughts during meditation? There's no doubt that Buddhist monks and gurus can, but we everyday people are hard-wired for distraction.

The more often we do this, the more we refine the experience, so over time, even short periods of meditation can be very effective. This type of rest for the mind is very important.

Andy Puddicombe, founder of Headspace (https://www.headspace.com/blog/ 2014/07/08/sleep-meditation/)

TYPES OF MEDITATION

Guided. Someone talks you through the experience. This can be great if you're new to meditation or you like to be led through a meditative journey. Listening to someone tell you what to focus on or visualize can help you tune out of any external distractions and activate intentions.

Vipassana. The one in which you're silent. Sitting in silence can be a struggle for most people – I always think this one's for hardcore meditators. If you can surrender to the experience and detach from your thoughts, attachments, aversions and distractions, it's said to be a profound experience.

Mantra. When you're repeating mantras, the vibrations of the words have a harmonizing effect. Repeating or chanting mantras can give you something to focus on so that your thoughts don't wander (as much) and the vibrations can have a sound healing effect on you.

Mindfulness. Focusing on the present moment and observing the details of what you're experiencing, without judgement. This can help if you're feeling anxious and your thoughts tend to lead you astray. Bringing your attention to what's real and in front of you, now, can guide you to feel more centred, calmer and appreciative of the small details you may not have noticed.

Active. Yoga, running, walking the dog, knitting, painting: anything that involves all of your focus and attention without you reaching for your phone or talking to anyone. For some people, sitting still for any amount of time trying to switch off their thoughts is their worst nightmare and can seem to make the thoughts even louder. If you find that your mind is quieter when you're doing something, make it mindful (see above).

Reiki. A self-healing treatment that could be considered as meditation. When you give yourself a reiki treatment, you are channelling high-vibration energies that may help you feel more balanced, with a calmer frame of mind. If you're initiated with reiki, you could give yourself a treatment for twenty to sixty minutes either first thing in the morning or in the evening, or both, to bookend your day with some good vibes.

*

If you want to develop your intuition, meditation can help you to rise above the distractions so that you can connect with your highest self. It may make it easier to pick up on the messages you're getting from working with the Moon. Think of meditation as a speaker/amplifier for your intuition because you can observe the subtle ways in which your intuition is trying to communicate with you, whether it's through sensations in your body or perceiving visions or messages, without noise from the outside world.

You will find Moon phase meditations to help you meditate with the Moon on pages 257–267.

If you have a history of mental illness such as schizophrenia, personality disorder or psychosis, consult your doctor or other qualified healthcare provider before beginning a meditation practice.

JOURNALLING:
WRITE YOUR
HEART OUT

'Do you have a daily practice?' Sabrina asked, during our Moon Club (an online membership platform) accountability call.

'Well, I meditate and do reiki treatments on myself as I'm going to sleep and sometimes in the morning. Oh, and I pull a Tarot or oracle card if I feel I need to, but it all depends on what's going on,' I replied, speaking through my laptop.

Sabrina was in LA and I was sitting in my bedroom on the other side of the Atlantic Ocean in Chelmsford. At the time, my morning rituals weren't consistent and I'd been explaining to Sabrina that I'd been feeling uncertain about how I wanted to move forward. It had been three months since I'd finally left my hairdressing job to focus on my spiritual business, 'Wolf Sister', but my new freedom had left me feeling overwhelmed and, well, stuck. I'd signed up to Moon Club because I wanted to make sure I had some kind of support network in place while I navigated this new territory of being totally self-employed. I'd known I'd miss the camaraderie of the salon, and this was my way of making sure that I was still part of a community.

Sabrina suggested I try doing something called Morning Pages: 'You just write three pages of whatever's in your head in the morning,' she explained.

'Umm, what size? A4?' Three pages sounded like a lot to write.

Morning Pages are a practice that I later discovered in *The Artist's Way* by Julia Cameron. In it, Julia describes writing the pages as 'a pathway to a strong and clear sense of self'.

The first time I did this, it was as if a fog lifted. I was blown away by the epiphanies that were coming through. 'You only get to know yourself by taking the time to observe and listen: it isn't all about taking action.' That's an excerpt from my first Morning Pages.

You've got to write to see what you're thinking. We have so many thoughts swirling around in our heads, but if we don't give them space to land, well, it gets crowded in there. Think of those cold winter mornings when it's a struggle to peel yourself out of your warm bed; the car needs de-icing and the windscreen is fogged but you're running late for work; you need to get moving and don't have time to wait for the screen to clear so you start driving slowly because you can't see what's ahead but you know the route. This is a really dangerous scenario but it's how I see us operating without meditation and journalling. This is what happens when you don't give yourself space to process what's going on in your life. I'm an advocate of medi-tation all day long (see page 122), but when you meditate, it's like you're pressing pause on your to-do list. It's all there wait-ing for you as soon as you've finished your meditation. When it comes to meditation and journalling, they're like two sides of BFF pendants. Together is better.

An argument or frustration with your partner, a disap-pointment at work, what to eat for breakfast, excitement about a new project you're planning, your thoughts on your best friend's move to the other side of the world, where to go on holiday, worries about your health, how to get out of your overdraft, the latest world crisis: you need somewhere to work it out. That's what journalling is for. It can be a pure and unadulterated stream of consciousness because nobody else will read it (as long as you keep it somewhere safe). You can write whatever you want. Free from judgement. Some days my pages are like a business meeting with myself, one long to-do list, then creative ideas pop in. Other days it's random ramblings in which I'm working out a challenging situation, and occasionally it's a pity party, with the world's tiniest violin playing for me. It's a safe space to give any rowdy thoughts somewhere to land so that I can see what I'm dealing with.

According to Dr Joe Dispenza, a pioneering lecturer, researcher and educator in the fields of neuroscience, epigen-etics and quantum physics, our thoughts are connected to our future. He explains that we think 60–70,000 thoughts a day and apparently 90 per cent of them are the same as yesterday's. Consider this: the same thoughts lead to the same choices and those choices perpetuate behaviours that result in the same

experiences, which cause the same emotions, which motiv-
ate the same thoughts. These repetitive thoughts effectively
hypnotize us into acting in a certain way so we unconsciously
do the same things and expect different results.

When I was preparing for *The Crystal Code* to be published,
I realized that nearly every sentence in my Morning Pages
began with 'I need to . . .' No wonder I felt overwhelmed: I
was brainwashing myself with the word 'need', over and over
again. The to-do list was relentless. These thoughts were spinning in my mind and it wasn't until I saw them on paper that
I was able to catch them out. Damn, girl: you need to stop
being so hard on yourself. That realization enabled me to flip
the script. From then on, every time I caught myself writing 'need', I'd either cross it out and write 'It would be good
if I could . . .' or I'd underline 'need' and ask myself, 'Do I
really need to do this?' This breakthrough led me to create an
affirmation for myself: 'It's safe for me not to do everything,
because it's already happening for me.' I wrote it on a bright
pink Post-it note so that I could be reminded of my new truth.
It's been liberating. I used this affirmation to create a sigil (see
page 217) on the new Moon and you'll never believe what happened: just after I'd inscribed the sigil on a piece of Labradorite, I received an email saying that one of my events had sold
out. I hadn't even had a chance to promote it.

Writing in my journal feels like I'm writing to my best
friend and business partner. She always gets me. It's a non-
negotiable part of my morning ritual. I look forward to it and
miss it when I don't get my pages in. My mind is so much
clearer for dedicating the time to this practice: it allows me

to be more productive when I need to be and I have some of my best ideas. If I can't journal for any reason, I usually try to catch up at another time in the day or before bed, and if I don't get to write at all, I'm okay with that, because maybe that's also part of the process. Doing Morning Pages has been a game changer for me.

PUTTING PEN TO PAPER

Curious to see what flows when you start writing your pages? Get an A4 notebook and a pen, and I'd recommend journalling first thing in the morning, before you're distracted by the day ahead. Aim to fill three sides of A4 paper, if you're doing the Morning Pages. Or you could journal after you've done a meditation, a Tarot/oracle card reading or a Moon ritual. When you're over-thinking something, try using this practice to decompress, especially if you haven't got someone to talk it out with. You may feel resistant to journalling, and it's natural to be apprehensive about what it might reveal. The truth ain't always sunshine and rainbows. It's often uncomfortable and raw. Bypass the censor that stops you writing how you really feel: what you don't own owns you. If you're stuck for what to write, you could just put, 'I don't know what to write.'

I find it easier to begin with 'Good morning, Pages, how are you?' so that I'm not intimidated by a blank page. I treat it as if I'm writing a letter that will never be read. The only rule is to fill all three pages. Treat your journalling time as a form of meditation: make sure you aren't checking your phone mid-sentence, breaking the flow to make a drink or finding other ways to distract yourself. Be prepared for some truth bombs to land. When you've been writing your Pages regularly for a while, you can use the journal to see if there are any patterns or links in your experiences with the Moon phases.

LET GRATITUDE BE YOUR ATTITUDE

When you show appreciation for what you have, you express gratitude, whether by saying thank you to someone, returning a kind gesture or acknowledging to yourself what's good in your life.

When we consciously *practise* gratitude, it can become a tool for transformation. Shift your focus from what you want and need to all of the things you've been given and already have in your life, whether it's your health, a job that pays the bills, a supportive family, your home, the new book you've been reading, a voice message from a friend that made you laugh, your bus turning up on time, the oracle card that made you feel confident about a decision you needed to make, finding a therapist who understands you, the price of the outfit you've had your eye on for ages dropping in the sale, your boss treating you to a drink after work, a babysitter for a date night, an appointment cancelled so that you have time for some self-care. Reflecting on what you're grateful for can be radical. Focusing on what you have can make you feel more abundant. What we appreciate appreciates.

Look out for signs that the universe has your back.

THE BENEFITS

Practising gratitude can help you feel more grounded in the here and now. It's easy to get caught up in the hustle, striving so hard to make something happen – just keeping up with everyday life can be a struggle some days – that you forget to stop and smell the roses. Gratitude guides you to see the positives in a situation: you consider what you have rather than what you may not. Like the friend who gives you a pep talk, it helps you zoom out and see the bigger picture.

Studies have found that acts of kindness and gratitude release large doses of dopamine, the feel-good hormone associated with bliss, motivation, concentration and euphoria. It motivates behaviours that will stimulate more dopamine. It can act as a natural anti-depressant, improves sleep quality and is said to have an analgesic effect to reduce physical pain. I know what you're thinking: where can I get some of that? It's worth noting that one of the reasons phone addiction is becoming an epidemic is due to the rush of dopamine we get when we receive a message or someone's tapped the little red heart on an Instagram post. We reach for our phones looking for distraction, connection or validation to give us a boost, which fades as we continue scrolling.

Showing appreciation is totally underrated. When you practise gratitude regularly, it can rewire your brain. A study at Indiana University, led by Prathik Kini, involved forty-three participants suffering from depression and anxiety. One group was assigned the task of writing gratitude letters to people in their lives, and the other group attended their usual counselling sessions but didn't write the letters. After three months, all of the participants had brain scans while they took part in a 'pay it forward' task. They were told that they'd been given a sum of money from a benefactor and were asked if they'd like to donate a portion of the gift to either a charity or a named person to express their gratitude. They were told that someone would actually receive the benefactor's money, minus the amount they chose to pay to their chosen charity.

The results of the scans showed that the more gratitude a participant felt, the more generous they were. The coolest discovery in the study, though, was that the group who'd performed the gratitude tasks reported feeling more grateful for two weeks after the 'pay it forward' exercise, and even months later, with gratitude-related brain activity showing in later scans. According to the researchers, these 'profound' and 'long-lasting' neural effects are 'particularly noteworthy'. Another study in 2005 reported that keeping a gratitude diary decreased depression by 30 per cent during the investigation.

This suggests that when gratitude is regularly felt it becomes your attitude. You could think of it as a muscle: the more you use it, the stronger it gets. You cultivate emotional intelligence, become resilient to stress and are more open to being kind, empathetic and supportive to others. I'm here for that.

SILVER LININGS

There are times when gratitude doesn't come easily: getting stung with a parking fine, being ghosted by the person you were supposed to be dating, missing a flight, an unexpected redundancy, a catastrophic miscommunication with a friend, tripping over a kerb and spilling coffee all over yourself. Those days when you wish you hadn't got out of bed, when you get stuck focusing on the things that aren't working: it can be so limiting. In the words of Oprah, 'There is no such thing as failure. Failure is just life trying to move us in another direction.' Look for the silver lining. Even if it's just a faint glimmer. I like to tune into what the situation is teaching me or consider the other opportunity it's creating: it's often a detour in a better direction. By shifting your perspective to the positive side of things, you're likely to find hope that there's a solution and act on it. That's where the magic really happens. Sometimes we need hindsight to realize it.

THE ART OF ATTRACTION

When you appreciate what you have, you create more of what you want. Gratitude is magnetic. It can help you attract your

Be thankful for what you have; you'll end up having more. If you concentrate on what you don't have, you will never, ever have enough.

Oprah Winfrey

next career path, a new romance or more abundance. When you have a better attitude, people respond to you differently. When I worked as a colour technician in a hair salon, there were times when I felt as if I was in a prison. I just wanted to be free to be doing healing sessions, Tarot readings and leading Moon ceremonies, but I had bills to pay. I couldn't support myself financially without my income from the salon (yet). I used to get so frustrated. It wasn't until I read *Big Magic* by Elizabeth Gilbert that I had a huge 'aha' moment: I couldn't expect my passion to pay the bills straight away. It's like having a baby and asking it to contribute towards the housekeeping. It doesn't work like that. You have the baby, nurture it and give it what it needs until it's grown-up, ready to be independent. So, when I was mixing an awkward client's colour, I'd take a deep breath and say to the dye, 'Thanks for supporting me to do what I love without financial fear,' then go to the client, smile and get to work. It shifted the dynamic and made the interaction a lot easier.

A little bit of gratitude can go a long way.

GET GRATEFUL

Here are some suggestions to get your dose of gratitude:

- Write a daily or weekly gratitude list in your journal.
- Add some emojis to your calendar before you set your alarm for the morning to symbolize what you're grateful for.

- Think of the things you're grateful for as you're about to fall asleep: it's the new version of counting sheep. Reflecting on what you're grateful for at the end of the day can help you feel more at ease with the day's events and leave it on a high.
- Set up a WhatsApp group with your friends and leave each other voice memos in the morning, saying what you're grateful for. It's such a lovely way to start the day.
- Involve your partner and/or children: share what you're grateful for before you eat your dinner together.
- Each month send thank-you letters or reach out to people who have inspired or supported you.
- When you're travelling abroad, make sure you know how to say thank you in the local language.

To supercharge your gratitude practice, make a date with the full Moon to reflect on all of the things you're grateful for (see Gratitude List, page 235, and Abundance Bath Ritual, page 242).

If you're working on self-love and body confidence, list what you love about yourself and your capabilities. If you're working on your finances, list the ways in which you're doing well, even if it's just finding a penny on the floor or a discount on your latest purchase, and the ways you're financially supported. If you're looking for a new home, list the things that are helping you find it, and when something falls through, try to trust that it's leading you somewhere even better. If you're going through a rocky patch in your romantic relationship, list the ways in which the other person supports you and consider what this situation is trying to show you.

And if you can't think of anything to be grateful for in the moment, what could you do to remedy that?

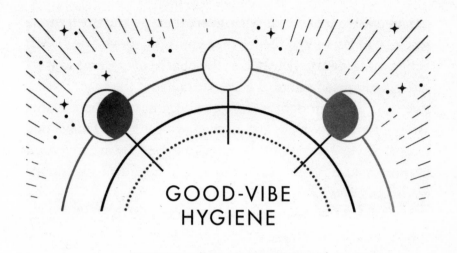

GOOD-VIBE HYGIENE

We *all* know that feeling of coming home after a bad day at work, wishing you could press ctrl-alt-delete on your life so that you can start again. The struggle can be oh-so-real, can't it? Sometimes all you need is an energy reset to help you decompress and leave the day behind. Cleansing your energy can be symbolic of letting go of what doesn't serve you, choosing not to hold grudges, practising compassion and, ultimately, letting the love back in. You can use these rituals to help you practise some good-vibe hygiene. It's like brushing your teeth but for your aura or space.

SMOKE CLEANSING

Recent scientific studies have found evidence that medicinal smoke can cleanse the air of harmful bacteria. Burning herbs has an uplifting effect: as with aromatherapy, the smell of the smoke can make you feel calmer and slow down your over-active mind. It also neutralizes the charge of positive ions by releasing large amounts of negative ions into the space. Negative ions are abundant in forests and jungles, where plants are photosynthesizing, and near moving water. This is one reason why spending time in nature can be so restorative, and keeping house plants can make a difference to your indoor environments.

You should be able to find the herbs and spices listed on the next page in your local supermarket or kitchen cupboard, and you could try growing them in your garden, then drying them. To enhance their magic powers, you could leave your store-bought ingredients to charge outside under the full Moon; if you're foraging or growing them yourself, pick them on the full Moon and leave them to dry naturally, perhaps in your airing cupboard. Use individually, or you could create your own blend. Keep your ritual ingredients in a designated place, such as your altar (see page 224) or a cupboard with your other witchy tools and goods.

If you'd like to learn more about using herbs, spices and flowers for spells, I recommend Semra Haksever's *Everyday Magic*.

You can use them individually, create your own blend, or I recommend checking out Star Child in Glastonbury: they create magical incense blends. Of course, if you can't make it to their shop in Glastonbury you can find them online.

• • • PLANT POWER • • •

Bay leaf: enhances psychic vision and is said to promote prophetic dreams. This protective herb can be used to attract good fortune and love; wards off negative energy.

Cardamom: believed to bring clarity to confusing situations. Potent for attracting a lover and increasing sexual confidence. This grounding spice can help you align with new opportunities.

Cinnamon: associated with fire, it is believed to fast-track intentions by increasing your magnetism. Use to attract love, abundance and money. Burn to purify and bless yourself or an area.

Ginger: this fiery root can inspire action and ignite passion. A potent aphrodisiac and stimulant. Can be used for concentration, motivation and power.

Juniper berries: beneficial for healing and purification. Soothing in times of emotional turbulence, and can support you to rise above challenging situations. Their protective energy can release negative attachments, helping you to move forward.

Lavender: a calming flower to quieten the mind, easing anxiety and restlessness. Enhances meditation and aids psychic awareness. Can be used as a blessing, to attract love and for protection.

Mint: an invigorating herb for new beginnings and success. Can be used for psychic protection; turns down the volume to distractions so that you can focus on your intentions.

Mugwort: associated with the Moon, as well as menstrual cycles. Activates the third eye and can enhance meditation, divination, lucid dreaming and astral projection.

Rose: a symbol of love, healing, loyalty, strength and romance. This heart-opening flower can guide you to be more compassionate, increases self-love and attracts fulfilling experiences.

Rosemary: an uplifting herb that can be used for focus, clarity and improving your memory. Well-known uses include purification and protection.

Sage (sustainable and ethical alternative to White Sage): this grounding herb can be used for healing, purification and protection rituals. Burn to clear and banish unwanted energy, and enhance divination.

How to Smoke-reset

You will need:

- A charcoal disc
- A heatproof bowl, ceramic burner or cauldron
- A small pair of tongs
- Dried herbs (see page 147) or incense
- A lighter
- A fan or feather
- Optional: sand or salt, to cover the base of the heatproof bowl

What to do:

- Hold the charcoal disc with the tongs and light the edge of the disc with a match or lighter. Once it's ignited, immediately place in the heatproof bowl. The disc will sparkle at first, then slowly begin to glow.
- Wait until the charcoal is glowing, then sprinkle over your dried herbs or incense, a small pinch at a time. In this case, less is better. It will create a lot of smoke: have a window open and don't sit too close to the fire alarm.
- You can either use a fan or feather to direct the smoke towards you or the object you are cleansing, or cup your hands through the smoke and draw it towards you, or hold an item that needs cleansing over the smoke for a few moments.

149

• • • SUSTAINABLE SMUDGING? • • •

Smudging, also known as saging, is the practice of using White Sage and Palo Santo (meaning 'holy wood' in Spanish) to get rid of unwanted energy you may have picked up from other people during the day, to shake off a bad mood, and cleanse the home or space. This is a sacred ritual to many peoples, Native Americans in particular. Traditionally used in ceremonies for purifying, cleansing the soul of negativity, and for blessings. It was illegal for Native Americans to practise their own religion until 1978; many were arrested and even killed for trying to keep their ways alive, including smudging. Now, with the increasing demand for White Sage and Palo Santo, there's reasonable concern about overharvesting and sustainability. These sacred plants and traditions are being exploited and misused. I was taught by a shaman how to smudge ceremonially, and I've used it in my personal practice with clients and for ceremonies.

We can still use smoke to cleanse, but the terms 'smudging' and 'saging' refer to the specific cultural practice used for spiritual healing, which belongs to indigenous peoples. Using smoke to cleanse isn't deep-rooted in spirituality or specific to a particular culture as smudging is.

ROOM RESET

I'd suggest doing a room reset in a new home, or working environment, if you've had unwanted guests, there's been an argument and stress, illness, or you've been struggling to concentrate or sleep. Start by opening the windows and doors, if possible, hold the heatproof dish with the smoking herbs – as long as it's safe to do so – and walk around the space, allowing the smoke to wash through the area. Use a fan to direct the smoke into the corners of the room. The open windows and doors allow stagnant energy to be released and invite fresh energy in.

Also try Waning Moon: Space-clearing Ritual (see page 248).

SALT BATHS

Salt is said to absorb negative energy; and it's one of the most accessible and sustainable tools that you could have in your self-care kit to clear your energy of any unwanted vibes. It's used by witches and in folk magic for protection and purification rituals. Having a salt bath to clear your energy can support good-vibe hygiene and may also have a grounding effect. If you've had a busy day, interacting with lots of people (offline/online), using a laptop or phone for a long time, you've been travelling or in a busy place, a salt bath can help to reset your energy and consciously disconnect you from the interactions you've been having so that you feel more connected to your body and can catch your breath. When you notice yourself feeling overwhelmed, anxious, exhausted, stressed, foggy-headed, and are finding it difficult to concentrate, a salt bath may help.

As with several spiritual practices, like crystal healing and reiki, the benefits haven't been scientifically proven but many people swear by the healing and restorative effects of salt baths.

A salt bath is one of my regular rituals, especially if I've been leading a Moon ceremony or workshop, or I've been working one-to-one with clients. I've noticed that whenever I don't have a salt bath after work, I feel too wired to sleep – the next day, it's as if I have a lunar hangover. No matter how late it is when I get home, I'll make sure I have a salt bath.

You will need:

- A bath
- 300g Epsom, Dead Sea or Himalayan salt
- Warm water
- Essential oils (optional) – you could use lavender, geranium, clary sage, rosemary or eucalyptus. Please check that they're suitable for use, especially if you have sensitive skin or allergies. Some essential oils are unsafe during pregnancy. Consult a medical professional for advice

What to do:

- Fill the bath with warm water and, as the water runs, add the salt.
- Ensure that the temperature and depth are comfortable for you.
- Relax and soak in the bath for at least fifteen minutes.
- When you're ready to get out, pull the plug but stay in the bath until all of the water has drained away. As you watch the level reducing, ask that any energy that doesn't belong to you be released; if you're releasing an attachment to someone else, ask that their energy returns to them and that the water nourishes them.

If you don't have a bath, you could use a salt scrub: massage it gently over your skin, and as you stand under the shower to rinse it off, visualize any energy that doesn't belong to you being washed away.

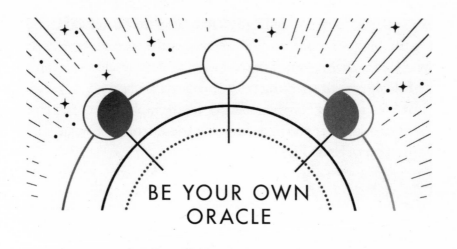

BE YOUR OWN
ORACLE

Working with Tarot or oracle cards is a form of divination (the practice of seeking knowledge of the future or the unknown by supernatural means). These tools have been shrouded in mystery and misconception for long enough. Perhaps you were fooled into thinking that only ultra-spiritual types and hipsters who possess magic powers are capable of using them, but these practices are for everyone. Especially you.

Some people may shy away from them: 'What if it tells me something I don't want to know or gives me bad news?' Well, the cards won't sugar-coat the truth (the Tarot especially), but they're only telling you what you already know deep down. Each card acts as a mirror: it's a reflection of your subconscious. It can shine a light on what's influencing you, holding you back, and what will support you to step into your highest potential.

The cards are a tool for personal development and trans-formation, like a portable cosmic adviser that's on call 24/7.

We can ask them for daily guidance, and they can help us to see the bigger picture so that we can gain a fresh perspective when we're feeling stuck or overwhelmed. One of my favourite side effects of working with the cards is clarity.

You've already got the answers you're looking for, but the cards can support you in excavating them from the noise and confusion of daily life.

WHAT IS THE TAROT?

A Tarot deck consists of 78 cards, which are divided into the Major Arcana (22 cards) and Minor Arcana (56 cards); 'arcana' means mystery, or secret. Each deck is unique and creators will depict the cards in their own way, but the fundamental elements are the same. The Major Arcana represent pivotal moments in our lives. It begins with the 'Fool' and takes us on a journey through to the 'World'; each card tells a story and has something to teach us about the human experience as we evolve. The Tarot is steeped in symbolism, with cards like the 'Devil', 'Death' and the 'Tower', which can be intimidating at first glance, but when you understand them, they aren't as scary as you initially thought. The Minor Arcana represents all the everyday details that are demanding our attention: each card indicates a situation, person, belief or behaviour that's influencing circumstances, and what can be done to help us step into our power. It has a similar format to a deck of playing cards: it's divided into four suits, ace through ten, with court cards for each suit, page, knight, queen and king. Each suit represents an element: swords = air; cups = water; wands = fire; pentacles (also represented as coins or crystals) = earth.

WHAT ARE ORACLE CARDS?

The difference between Tarot and oracle cards is that oracle cards don't necessarily have a particular structure. They're often an intuitive/creative expression of the artist and author inspired, for example, by unicorns, goddesses, angels, animals, plants, crystals, mermaids, astrology, food . . . Oracle cards can be more accessible than the Tarot; the messages may seem more light-hearted and encouraging. The Tarot may come across as tough love because it can be so specific as to what it's addressing.

HOW TO CHOOSE A DECK

Myth says you should be given your deck, and as thoughtful as that may be, my friend, you could end up waiting a long time for that to happen. Unless you choose a deck and put the link on your birthday wishlist.

Whether it's a Tarot or oracle deck you go for, it's important to choose one with imagery you like and are drawn to. You can buy Tarot and oracle decks from bookshops, boutiques and the most mystical place you can think of: scroll through Instagram to see what your favourite mystics are working with. Some incredible artists/intuitives self-publish their own decks, which can usually be found online.

HOW TO USE TAROT/ORACLE CARDS

Ideally, I'd recommend getting comfortable in a place where you won't be disturbed, but don't let that hold you back if you want to check in with the cards. You could do a meditation or simply take a few slow, deep breaths, to quieten your mind and get into the mood, before you pick up the deck.

Start by shuffling the cards. You don't need to do your best impression of a Las Vegas casino croupier to get a golden answer from your deck. There's no such thing as being 'bad' at shuffling when you're doing this. Use it as an act of mindfulness to help you feel connected with the present moment and tune into the situation that you're seeking guidance with.

Before you choose a card, think of the question you'd like to ask. The key to getting the most insightful answers from the cards is asking a question that's expansive rather than looking for a definitive answer. Expecting yes or no is limiting and can make the answer tricky to read.

Suggested questions:

- What will support me today?
- How am I holding myself back?
- What is the truth in this situation?
- What lesson am I learning at the moment?
- How can I step into my power?
- What is my intuition trying to show me?
- As my higher self, what do I need to be aware of today?

If you keep asking your friends for advice about a particular issue, try it out on the cards.

Some people like to cut the deck in a particular order with the left hand; others like to spread the cards (with the backs facing upwards) in front of them on the table, or create a fan with them before choosing the card they are drawn to. Certain cards may catch your eye or you can run your fingers over the deck until you feel a magnetic pull towards one. Perhaps you're the kind of person who always goes for the card at the top of the deck or for the one that's hidden behind a cluster. One of my friends chooses a card that 'jumps' out while she's shuffling. You do you: pull the cards however you like.

As long as you have a clear intention with the question you're asking before you pull the card, it doesn't matter how you shuffle or choose them.

Hold tight. I know it will be tempting to dive straight to the index of the guide book or consult Google to find out what your card is saying, but slow down and take time to look at the card: what's happening in the image? Does it have a message or a title that's thought-provoking? What are your first impressions? Does it relate to anything specific that's been happening for you? Use this as an opportunity to flex your intuition, write some notes, then see what the card is 'officially' saying. Chances are, it won't be far from what you've already noted.

Considering how many cards there are in a Tarot or oracle deck, it's likely that over time you'll have a few familiar cards that keep popping up for you – a.k.a. stalker cards. Ugh, that one again? The cards that make you roll your eyes are usually enforcing a message you aren't acting on (deep down you know you need to) or affirming where you are at the moment. We don't really choose the cards: the cards choose us. If you put back a card because you don't understand or like what it was saying, get it out again and let its message simmer. There's a reason why it came up for you. Journal about it and what it brings to mind. The more challenging cards are an opportunity to go deeper, to where we really get to know ourselves. When it's a card that resonates or we like what it's saying because it's giving us a cosmic high-five, we tend to bypass the depth of the message. It's like, 'Yeah, I get it,' and you move on without any reflection. We always benefit from reflecting, even when it feels as if we're in the flow lane.

How Often Should You Use Them?

In this book, you'll find lunar-inspired spreads for the Moon phases to help you reflect and process what's coming up for you. Use the cards as part of your Moon rituals so that you can tune into what the Moon is trying to show you. Use the cards to find your own answers. I also recommend pulling a daily card to ask: what will support/ground/inspire/empower me today? Keep your card of the day or a stalker card on your altar (see page 224) or somewhere you'll see it frequently as a friendly reminder.

MOON PHASE: ORACLE SPREADS

No two Moons are ever the same. What we experience is also influenced by the other planetary transits, like retrogrades, eclipses or astrological aspects (the angles between the planets). It's easy enough to check in with your horoscopes and see what your favourite astrologers are saying about the cosmic weather but they're often generalized for the collective. If you want something more personal, to find out what each Moon phase is saying for *you*, grab your Tarot or oracle deck and flex your intuition with these layouts to get a personal lunar reading

How To Use These Spreads

You can use oracle spreads, according to the current Moon phase. You can do them on their own as a Moon ritual or alongside other Moon rituals (see pages 213–256) in this book. Sit somewhere quiet, where you won't be disturbed or distracted, and create a sacred space (page 17) for yourself. You can do a meditation before using the spread or simply take a few slow, deep breaths to help you feel more relaxed and quieten your mind for the reading. Shuffle your deck, and before you pull each card, ask the questions according to the spread you're working with. Place the cards in the order and positions that are illustrated in the following diagrams. Turn the cards over and have them face up as you put them down so that you can see them all together. When you pull cards individually, as a daily single card, you may see a snapshot of a situation; with more than one card, you can start to see a bigger picture and the various influences at play. Spend some time reflecting on the messages from the cards and your first impressions of what they may mean for you. Journal about the cards and how they may apply to your situation; this can help if you're confused by your interpretation. You'll be keen to look up the cards' meanings but, first, try to use your intuition to feel into what the cards are saying to you; then look up the cards if you need to. Use these Moon phase spreads on your own or with friends so that you can share perspectives on the interpretations of the cards' messages; sometimes the answers are clearer after we've talked about how they could apply to us.

NEW MOON

New Moons are all about new beginnings and setting intentions; you can use this spread to tune into what you need to know about the new cycle to align with it.

Card 1. What is this new Moon opening/awakening for me?

Card 2. What will support me during this Moon cycle?

Card 3. How can I stay open to receiving fresh opportunities?

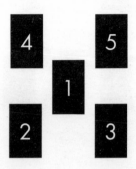

WAXING MOON

Waxing Moons can be about taking action. Use this spread to clarify what you need to focus your attention on and the steps you could take to help things move forward in your life.

Card 1. What do I need to focus on?

Card 2. How am I holding myself back?

Card 3. What action do I need to take?

Card 4. How can I make space for what will support me?

Card 5. What will make things flow more easily?

FULL MOON

Full Moons can be an intense time as certain aspects in your life become hard to ignore. Use this spread to understand what's culminating and how to surrender to what it brings up for you.

Card 1. Which area of my life is this full Moon illuminating for me?

Card 2. What intention has manifested with this full Moon?

Card 3. Where can I invite more love, pleasure and fun into my life?

Card 4. What's been triggering me?

Card 5. How can I stay grounded?

Card 6. How am I being supported?

Card 7. What do I need to stop trying to control?

Card 8. How can I embrace change?

Card 9. A message from my higher self?

WANING MOON

Waning Moons are an opportunity to release and make space for something new, as the Moon wanes towards the new Moon. Use this spread to tune into what it's time to let go and how to use what you've learnt during this Moon cycle to make you wiser and stronger.

Card 1. What habit/belief/relationship/situation am I ready to let go?

Card 2. What has this experience taught me?

Card 3. What do I need to forgive?

Card 4. How can I be kinder to myself (and others)?

Card 5. What can I do to heal myself?

Card 6. What will support me to move forward?

DARK MOON

The dark Moon is like the space between an ending and a new beginning; it's a time for stillness and reflection rather than taking specific action. Use this spread to help you reflect on the messages that this Moon phase has for you.

Card 1. What have I achieved?

Card 2. What do I need to press pause on?

Card 3. How can I surrender to the unknown?

Card 4. A message from my inner high priestess?

MANIFEST WITH
THE MOON

One of the main reasons that people are paying attention to the Moon is because of its potential to support a manifestation process. In the age of social media we're constantly seeing what we could have that we haven't got already, and so much is accessible at just a tap away. We'll take all the help we can get to create a lifestyle on our terms. Gardeners and farmers aren't the only ones who've been utilizing the benefits of lunar power: throughout history, witches, pagans, shamans and Wiccans have celebrated the phases of the Moon and harnessed its power for healing, transformation and celebration.

In spirituality, manifestation occurs when you receive something that you've requested from the universe. Here we'll take inspiration from the way in which these cultures work with lunar cycles to improve our chances of making good things happen in our lives. A lot of people focus on the new and full Moon for manifestation but the other phases are just as beneficial to the process. If you've already dipped your toe into manifestation but it's been missing some juice, align your process with the Moon phases.

It can take up to six months for something to manifest fully, which is also the time it takes for the full Moon to find its way into the corresponding zodiac sign, preceding a new Moon. So, if you set an intention during the Aries new Moon, you may see it come to life when the full Moon is in Aries.

Here's a simple breakdown of the process:

- New Moon: set intentions
- Waxing Moon: take action
- Full Moon: celebrate your achievements, practise gratitude and upgrade
- Disseminating Moon: reprogramme limiting beliefs
- Waning Moon: release and forgive
- Dark Moon: rest and reflect

From new Moon to full Moon, set your intention on the new Moon, then over the coming days build up towards taking more action. Work with the full Moon to practise gratitude, celebrate, launch a new project and/or do something that represents upgrading your life. Full Moons are a powerful time to set intentions and are supported by the abundant energy of the Moon during this phase. If you miss setting your intentions on the new or full Moon, don't let superstition restrict you. This is just a guide: you can set intentions at any time that feels right for you.

From full Moon to new Moon: after the full Moon has

peaked, this is the time to start conserving your energy and slow down. Use this energy until the dark Moon for releasing, reprogramming and going into a resting phase. Reflect on what you've learnt during the Moon cycle, what's challenged and encouraged you, your achievements, inspirations, lessons and breakthroughs.

WHAT IS MANIFESTATION?

You may have heard the urban legend about the person who read a Law of Attraction book, wrote a cheque to themselves for a million pounds and woke up the next day to find out they'd had a windfall. That is what's commonly known as manifestation, but I've never met anyone it's happened to like that.

People are harnessing the Law of Attraction to transform their lives – or at least get a sold-out dress for half the retail price in their size. In case I lost you at Law of Attraction: it means we attract energy that's a likeness. Simply put, if you think good things, then good things will happen to you and vice versa. While I don't necessarily believe that 'bad' things happen to us because we're in a bad mood or stuck in a rut, I do believe that energy flows where attention goes. If you're constantly saying things like, 'I don't have enough money,' subconsciously you'll keep making decisions based on that belief, which can perpetuate this perceived reality. We like to prove ourselves right, after all.

The Fundamentals of Manifestation

- Set an intention (ask for what you want).
- Believe in it and the universe will work its magic to bring it to you.

This is all quite surface level and we'll be talking later about what needs to happen to take it deeper. I know people who've used the basics of this practice to get parking spaces, tickets to sold-out events, a free session with a healer and a hotel upgrade.

For the sceptics at the back: of course anyone can set an intention and make something happen if they put their mind to it, but when you're manifesting, it's all about getting into alignment with what you'd like to happen in your life. Mindset plays a big role, and the choices you make are vital, but you're also calling in the support of a benevolent force to help things align for you. As humans, we have a tendency to do things the hard way but when you're asking for back-up from the universe, you may be pleasantly surprised at how easily something can find its way to you.

Some manifesting rhetoric suggests you just need to visualize and think positively to get what you want, but I'd say that's spiritual bypassing with a dose of privilege for good measure. Just because you want something doesn't necessarily mean you're entitled to or ready for it. It isn't just about manifesting material things we don't need. We're here to use all of this to make a difference, and not just in our own lives.

You are here to experience all of your feelings: if you're

having a shit day, that's okay. It's unlikely that you'll keep attracting undesirable situations just because you're in a low mood you haven't been able to shake. It's your actions and choices that influence the outcome. Dust yourself off when you're ready and take note of the lessons from what's been happening. We need to play our part, take responsibility, learn and do the work. Otherwise where's the sense of achievement? To get to the juicy stuff, we need to roll up our sleeves and go deeper.

In the summer of 2016, I described my dream day as part of a manifestation ritual. At the time I was still working as a hairdresser four days a week, doing my healing work and leading ceremonies on the side. I was constantly burnt out from trying to spin too many plates. I was living with my boyfriend in a flatshare and we'd been talking about buying our first home. I wrote down the ultimate day that I wanted to live and described its details, from what I'd have for breakfast, to where I was, who I'd interact with and my feelings throughout it. I included that I wanted to be paid to write. I wasn't specific about what exactly I'd write about but in my mind it would be monthly Tarotscopes (like horoscopes but using the Tarot) or some kind of column for a magazine: I was calling in some steady income to support me to leave hairdressing. Little did I know that I'd be approached the following year by a literary agent and begin writing my first book, *The Crystal Code*.

We grow into our manifestations. It isn't like ordering a dress online and it landing on your doorstep within twenty-four hours. There are limiting beliefs that require reprogramming, and comfort zones we need to move beyond to make the good stuff happen.

Yes, there are times when it can seem that you've had a fast-track manifestation but you were most likely already working on it without even realizing.

What would you like to experience in your life? You could think of it as a goal or something you're aiming for. It could be an achievement, overcoming a challenge or moving on from a trauma. It could be a new relationship, or bringing the spark back to an existing one. It could be cultivating a more harmonious relationship with your in-laws or housemates. It could be learning to love yourself. It could be a new job or career opportunities. It could be more money in the bank as you pay off your debts. It could be somewhere to live – perhaps you'd like to invest in a property one day or just find somewhere that you can put roots down for longer than a few months. It's got to be realistic. I'm not going to suggest anything health or fertility-related because this isn't something I have experienced.

There's something that a lot of people miss out when it comes to manifestation: what feelings do you want to experience? Because it's the feelings we're chasing, just as much as the outcome.

Don't put pressure on yourself to manifest the big things overnight: what you're calling in might be a slow burn but it will have strong roots. Not seeing results? Thinking about giving up? Here's a thought: the last thing to grow on a fruit tree is the fruit. You'll probably get thrown some curve balls, and there'll be twists and turns you could never have antici-pated, but it's leading you towards something wonderful.

At this point, you're probably eager to know how you can access your own manifesting gold mine. It's a process: lots of people have their own spin on how it works but this is my formula that I've used to manifest most of the good things in my life.

1. Set intention

What would you like to experience in your life? It really helps if you can be specific; rather than just saying you want to be happy, for example. Happiness isn't easy to quantify. Instead tune into what would make you happy. Could it be a holiday, reducing your days at your current job to make space for your side hustle, going to a yoga class once a week, spending some quality time with someone you care about or moving to the countryside?

A little while ago, my friend Jess sent me a message on WhatsApp and told me she was struggling to find some-where to live. She'd been living somewhat nomadically and was craving a sense of stability.

'You need to be specific with what you're looking for so that you can send out a clear signal to the universe,' I explained, before asking her some questions. 'Where do you want to live, who do you want to live with and how much rent do you want to pay?'

Jess replied, and we went back and forth getting into all of the details, such as she wanted her new home to have a gas cooker and a garden. Two days later, my phone pinged with a message from Jess: she'd found a place that ticked off all of the things she'd asked for in our text conversation and she was moving in soon.

When it comes to manifesting a relationship, it's really important to home in on how you'd like to feel with that person and the ways in which you'd be open to the relationship evolving, rather than what that person may look like, the car they drive or their job. Hands up if you've been on a date with someone who seemed to tick so many boxes but the chemistry wasn't there. Remember: call in the feelings as much as the specifics. And don't be so specific that you include a name, like your office crush. You can describe the qualities you're drawn to in that person but don't put all your focus on them. When it comes to crushes, we often see what we want to see and that person might not live up to those perceptions in reality. Be mindful of who/what you wish for.

If you're manifesting something career-related, reflect on what the opportunity may look like. Who would you be working with and how do you feel about working with them? What would the interactions or working relationships be like? How much would you want to be paid? How long would your ideal commute take? How many days a week would you prefer to work? Are there any other perks or responsibilities you'd like in this situation?

Stuck on the specific details? Reflect on the things you've enjoyed in the past, and would like more of, and the things you'd rather not repeat: they can help you work out what's non-negotiable for you.

You can manifest money and opportunities, but be clear on what that money is for rather than just plucking a number out of the sky. For me, manifesting isn't about calling in material possessions unless that will enhance my life in some way – money to invest in a new laptop so that you can start an online venture, or a pay rise so that you can afford to see a therapist.

Check in with *why* you'd like your intention to become reality because if it's coming from a place of ego, to compete against someone else or to gain external validation, you may find yourself on a bumpy road: the universe is always trying to get you to the higher ground.

To start with, focus on *one* area of your life that you'd like to work on: relationships, career, home, finances or well-being. If you really don't know what you want and are feeling stuck in your life, I'd recommend calling in clarity and support to help you discover what your next move could be. You can either create an empowerment (a statement of intention), like 'I'm ready to take things to the next level' or 'I release my fear and confusion so that I can receive love/opportunities', or write a list of feelings and intentions based on that situation. This is the foundation of your unlimited day: begin to imagine what it could look like.

A lot of manifestation practices encourage us to write lists but I think we've got enough to-do lists going on in our lives. Rather than reinforce something that hasn't become reality, writing about your unlimited day can help you recognize it when it all comes to fruition and helps you to make decisions to support the process. With the unlimited day, you can try it for size as you're imagining it, then decide if that's what you really want or you need to tweak it. Write it as if it's already happening and describe it as if you're living it. Read it back to yourself. How does it feel? It may seem daunting, like being on a rollercoaster upside down, waiting for the drop that will make you scream but is exhilarating at the same time. If you're feeling excited about it, you're on the right track.

What you're calling in needs to be believable: if you don't believe it's possible for you, you'll need to rewind and set a more realistic intention. For example, you're not going to manifest a mansion with a swimming pool if you're living with your parents and struggling to contribute to the bills because you're up to your eyeballs in debt. Your first manifestation step could be to repay your loans and clear your credit cards. Once you're in a more stable financial situation, you can consider where you'd like to live, according to your budget, then work your way towards the mansion, if that's still what you want. This way, you should see results quicker.

Our limiting beliefs can really restrict our powers of manifestation, so if you don't believe you could do the job of your dreams or be loved, for example, I'd suggest setting an intention of an opportunity to see that it's possible. This could come in the form of a mentor, therapist or someone from a similar background who's making it happen in their life so you have proof that it's possible.

After you've written the story of your unlimited day, sign it at the end with 'I'm open to this or something better so that we can all rise together.' This statement affirms your trust in the process and that you aren't trying to manipulate anyone else to get what you want.

You need to write it only once, unless you want to edit something. Trust that once is enough to activate it. If you change your mind, you can rewrite it. This work isn't set in stone.

To set your intention you can either write it as an empowerment on a Post-it note, create some artwork inspired by it and keep it somewhere you can see it, programme a crystal with it, or create a sigil (see page 217). With your unlimited day, you can burn it, bury it or put it in with the recycling, keep it on your altar (page 224), under your pillow, in your journal, or seal it in an envelope to open at a later date.

2. Identify limiting beliefs and reprogramme

Think of your intention as the tip of the iceberg: all of your subconscious beliefs around what you're asking for lurk below the surface. You may have noticed a couple bubble up as you were writing your intentions. To some extent, our thoughts create our reality, not entirely because we can only imagine how random and erratic the world would be (it's wild enough out there as it is), but if you keep thinking the same things, you brainwash yourself into thinking they're true and will make decisions based on those beliefs. If you have a fear based on a previous trauma or disappointment, or tell yourself that whatever you want you won't get, or remember possible negative repercussions, have low self-worth and keep putting yourself down, it's harder for your intention to gain full traction.

Here's an example of a limiting belief: you're bored with your job, the wages aren't a true reflection of what you bring to the table and you've been wondering if you should send out your CV to see what's around. However, you've got it easy in many ways, and there's a lot going on in your personal life so you don't want to add any more pressure. The limiting belief: a new job equals stress.

On an energetic level you're sending mixed signals to the universe. You're saying, 'I want this *but* I don't want to fail, get hurt (again), lose out, let anyone down, can't afford it or don't have time.' These limiting beliefs can carry more weight than the intention, so the universe will send you opportunities to see things differently until you're ready to say *yes* wholeheartedly to what you've been asking for.

You may have noticed that you keep repeating a pattern and finding yourself in the same situation: there's a belief that's reinforcing it. It's time to break the cycle.

Journalling (see page 131) can support you to identify limiting beliefs. Take some time to write about what you'd like to manifest, how you feel about it, any experiences from the past (or that have happened to someone you know) that could be making you apprehensive and holding you back. Once you've uncovered that belief you can weed it out and reprogramme. Get a highlighter pen to underline anything that stands out. The simplest way to reprogramme the limiting belief is to call it out and reframe it to create an empowerment.

For example:

I'm not good enough . . .
becomes
You've got this.

You could write the empowerment on a Post-it note or turn it into a piece of artwork that you'll see regularly, create a sigil (see page 217), or use it as a password so that you're connecting with it daily. To go deeper with this, you could have a session with a qualified hypnotherapist to support you to reprogramme and integrate new ways of believing in yourself.

Limiting beliefs come not only from our own experiences: we can pick them up from the people we're with each day. Jim Rohn, entrepreneur, motivational speaker and author, said, 'You are the average sum of the five people you spend the most time with.' This means that who you interact with and the conversations you have can weigh heavily on your manifesting abilities. Put it this way, if you're hanging out with people who are always gossiping and complaining but have all of the excuses under the Sun for not improving things for themselves, it may be harder for you to believe it's possible for you to break free. This can apply to friends who work as freelancers and are always saying they're broke, single friends who keep saying that the dating scene is a minefield and all of the 'good' ones are taken, coupled friends who seem unfulfilled in their long-term relationships, parents who say that their life/career is on hold now that they've had a baby, or you work in an industry that's focused on appearance and youth, where there's a limited shelf life for success. Or – this one's juicy: you can't have it all. That doesn't have to be your reality. *What if you can have it all?*

Now, I'm not saying you need a friendship detox and should dramatically cut these people out of your life with immediate effect, but if any relationships are toxic, abusive or one-sided, you know what you need to do when it comes to creating some boundaries. I'd suggest checking in with how the conversations you've been having with these people are supporting you and reinforcing your restrictions. Either avoid having certain conversations or spend less time with them and make an effort to spend more with people you admire, who are walking their talk.

It isn't always easy to find inspirational people to befriend, especially if you have social anxiety, are too busy, can't get a babysitter, live in the middle of nowhere or don't have the funds to go to a talk or workshop. Thank goodness for the internet! We're spending more and more time on our phones so why not use them to our benefit? Podcasts are an incredible way to be part of a conversation that you wouldn't usually be privy to. Listen to podcasts that encourage you to see the world in ways that feel empowering, informative, supportive, and help you to feel less alone.

I know a lot of people have a love-hate relationship with social media, but if it's used in the right way, it's a wonderful place for connection and expansion. If you're trying to cultivate more self-acceptance and body positivity, unfollow accounts that make you feel bad about yourself and tune into the ones that are inclusive, championing self-love and diversity. If you're trying to get a project off the ground, but some of the accounts you're following are triggering imposter syndrome or comparison, mute them so you can focus on your own lane. Search hashtags for your interests or check out who the people you admire are engaging with. The joy of Instagram is that you can curate a stream of cheerleaders. Use it to strengthen new perspectives so that you're absorbing content that supports you to level up. When it comes to this app, you decide who has your attention. Just because someone is following you, you don't have to follow them if you don't want to. It's a great place to find new friends who share the same interests and discover people you wouldn't necessarily meet in your neighbourhood.

3. The F-word

Forgiveness isn't always easy but if you're holding on to resentment, whether it's towards another person or yourself, it can make it harder for your manifestations to come in. The F-word can be triggering so hear me out: this isn't to condone something that someone has done to you in the past or perhaps that you're carrying guilt or shame about. Forgiveness is the moment when you choose to let it go in order to move forward. It's an opportunity to embody the lessons from this experience and see how it's made you stronger and wiser, whether it's a grudge that you're holding against a boss, a parent who let you down, an ex who cheated on you or a friend who stole from you. Set yourself free. Call back your power by leaving it/them in the past. Letting it go is part of making something happen. (See page 246 for Cord-cutting Ritual.)

4. Align with the energy

Some people wonder why their manifestations aren't coming through, and it's often because they're just going through the motions of manifesting, missing the feelings that will fuel it. Perhaps you're reciting your wish list or visualizing your manifestation coming to fruition every night before you go to bed. It's become another chore with no thrills. Think of a time when you were newly single, totally feeling yourself, not in a hurry to get into a new relationship, and your milkshake was bringing all the boys or girls into the yard. Fast-forward to a year later and you've kissed more than your fair share of frogs (or should I say ghosts? That's what they keep doing) and you're losing the faith. You are so much more magnetic when you're energetically aligned with your intentions.

Here are a few suggestions to help you get aligned.

Playlist
I love creating playlists on Spotify that help me to get in the mood. I've got a money-abundance playlist that has songs about – you guessed it – money. It makes me feel psyched for dealing with my bank accounts and taxes or when work has been a little slow. Listening to those songs makes me feel more confident about my situation, even if the cash isn't flowing into my bank account (yet). What would be on your manifesting playlist?

Crystals

Crystals are very helpful when it comes to aligning yourself with new energy. Every crystal has its own frequency, and when we connect with them, we tune into their energy through a process called entrainment. You'll be aware of entrainment in action when you spend time with certain people and you're aware of how your mood changes when you're with them. It can go in more than one way: uplifted or drained, or somewhere in between. Crystals have the same effect but on a subtler level. When you choose a crystal to support your manifestation process and work with its energy through meditation or keeping it close to you, it can help you to get into the frequency of what you'd like to experience.

Yes

Say yes to the things and opportunities that will support your vision for the future. Think: what would the ultimate version of yourself choose to be doing today? Focus on what you want and say no to anything that isn't supportive.

Receive

When you're manifesting, there's an element of calling in support from external forces. You can't always do it alone. There needs to be a balance of giving and receiving. If you won't accept support in your daily life – burning yourself out because you refuse to delegate, always picking up the bill, insisting you're okay when you're struggling – how can you receive anything when your hands are full? When you're going above and beyond to try to make something happen, you're often choosing the hard way of doing things and aren't trusting that sometimes these things can happen without you even having to lift a finger. You know how good it feels when you've done something thoughtful for a friend or helped someone in need: let someone else try on those rewarding feelings for size. Let them be there for you. Give yourself a day off; ask for help; get your partner to cook dinner (or order a takeaway); employ a cleaner; go on a retreat; surrender to your best friend treating you to lunch; have a massage; practise being in receiving mode to help you attract more abundance.

Embody
Your physiology informs your psychology, which basically means that your posture can influence the way you're thinking and feeling. Try this: slouch for a few minutes and check in with how you feel. Then stand up straight with your hands on your hips and hold your head high for a few minutes. Do you notice a difference in the way you feel afterwards? With the latter you're more likely to feel confident and strong, which can elevate your thoughts and decisions. Yoga can be a wonderful way to embody a mood or feeling based on the sequence of asanas. There was a time when I'd been told at short notice that my boyfriend and I needed to move out of the place where we'd been living. As you can imagine, it was pretty stressful and we could have gone to stay with my boyfriend's parents, but that wasn't ideal for various reasons. After having a mini meltdown, I set my intention of what I'd like the outcome to be and then, to help me relax, I followed a yoga sequence on YouTube. I felt so much better after twenty

minutes of practice. A few hours later, a friend called to say that he'd heard we needed somewhere to stay and could use his empty apartment, which was being sold. You could call it a coincidence or see it as the result of getting aligned.

Gratitude

Align with your intentions by being grateful for what you already have and what's happening in your life right now. The small wins add up. Sometimes you've got to hunt for the silver linings but they're there if you look for them. Rejection is protection: if something hasn't worked out in the way you'd expected, trust that it happened for a good reason and is getting you into alignment for something better.

5. Take steps towards it

When we're trying to manifest something, the task can seem too big. You think of other people who've achieved something similar and, of course, they've made it look so easy. You want what they've got now. I don't believe in overnight successes. Unfortunately, we don't get to see enough of what goes on behind the scenes, and perhaps you've only recently discovered someone who looks as if they're slaying it but you've missed the part of their life where their romantic life was a disaster and they were juggling three jobs.

Social media tends to be a curated showreel that tricks us into thinking that everyone's got life locked down. But, we all have to start somewhere so why not take the first step today? Write a list of things you can do towards your goal, make sure they're doable, and schedule in the time to make them happen. Send the email; download the app; apply for the course; arrange the time off work; order the book; set up an Instagram account; create a Pinterest board for inspiration; buy a domain name for your new business; arrange a call with a life coach or therapist. Put your best foot forward. To achieve anything worth having, there will always be trial and error. Failures. There will be times when you feel challenged, overwhelmed and confused. You will need to step beyond your comfort zone at times. This is all in the name of personal growth.

There will be moments of frustration because your manifestation hasn't happened for you yet. Is there space for it to come into your life? You may be wondering why you aren't getting your dream opportunities but perhaps you've been working overtime at a job you don't love and you haven't the energy to do anything else. Or you're too busy people-pleasing so you don't have any spare time to pursue your new interests. You need to schedule time to nurture your manifestation process.

Rather than waiting for your intentions to manifest and telling yourself that when X, Y and Z happen you'll take a leap of faith, do something about it today. What would you be doing if your manifestation became reality? Act as if it's already happening. Some people might say, 'Fake it until you make it,' but I like to think of it as getting into alignment with something that's on its way. Rather than waiting for the perfect conditions, just go for it, in the ways that are available to you now. Actions can speak louder than words.

6. Surrender

Just because you think you're ready for what you're manifesting that doesn't mean he/she/it is ready too. I like to sign off my manifestation intentions with 'I'm open to this or something better so that we can all rise together' because, first, I'm honouring others in the process. Second, I'm letting go of attachment to the outcome. And, last, I'm a human with limiting beliefs. It allows the universe to take charge in case I'm playing too small. Some people seem to manifest what they want overnight but, whether they knew it or not, things were playing out long before they struck it lucky. It can seem super-frustrating and you may be tested with comparisons, battling an existential crisis, spiralling into over-thinking about what others may have that you haven't. It's like getting stuck in quicksand: don't do it to yourself. If you try to control the outcome too much, you restrict the flow of what can come to you or are too distracted by what you think you should be doing that you miss an opportunity to take an easier route. Think of it this way: if you're doing everything you can to make it happen, do you have a spare hand to receive what you're hoping for? Allow yourself to be supported; don't be too shy to ask for help. When you surrender and say yes to being supported, you're also in receiving mode.

Manifestation is a fine balance of taking actions that support the process but equally allowing it to come to you, rather than chasing it. It may feel like a friend who said she'd be ready to go out in five minutes over an hour ago, but when you finally get to your destination, you have the best time together. Chill out, get yourself a drink and put the tunes on. Embrace and enjoy where you are: find the beauty in that moment. Don't try to rush or force what isn't ready yet. If your manifestation process is taking you on a detour, trust that it's guiding you towards something better.

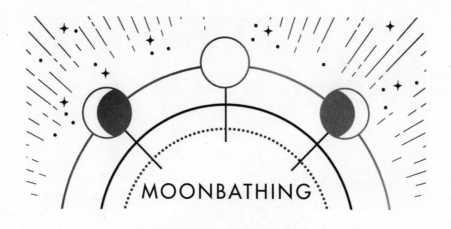

MOONBATHING

Moonbathing is like sunbathing, except you're soaking up moonbeams instead of the Sun's rays. You won't get a bronzed glow but, just as you may feel recharged after topping up your tan, moonbathing is an opportunity to slow down, reflect and commune with the Moon.

The Sun's personality is renowned to be masculine; its energy radiates outwards and is associated with initiation and action. The Moon is all about the feminine aspects of being human. It's associated with reflection, receptivity, surrender and experiencing your feelings. When we align with the Moon, we're reclaiming these innate feminine traits. You have perhaps been hanging back when it comes to things demanding your attention.

You could think of moonbathing as an act of self-care: tuning out of the hustle and getting down with the Moon for a dose of stillness before aligning with your next move.

HOW TO MOONBATHE

You can moonbathe outside (if it's safe to do so) or indoors by a Moon-facing window. It's up to you if you want to get naked or wear something loose and comfortable. You may want to wrap up warm if you're going outside and it's cold.

Moonbathing is simple. After sunset, lie down in a place where you'll be exposed to the Moon's energy.

If you don't live somewhere with easy access to the Moon, due to your environment or living conditions, your second-best option is to visualize the Moon, with a little help from a piece of moonstone (if you have it) placed on the centre of your forehead, to connect with your third eye.

Either way, follow this visualization to soak up some moonlight.

Guided Moonbathing Meditation

- Lie on your back somewhere comfortable where you won't be disturbed.
- You could put on a playlist or simply set a timer, depending on how long you'd like to moonbathe.
- Close your eyes and imagine the Moon or gaze at it, if you can see it.
- Bring your awareness to your breathing: breathe in to the count of six and exhale to the count of seven. Follow this cycle until you feel calm and relaxed, then allow your breath to flow at a slow and natural pace.

- Visualize the Moon's energy shining down on you as you absorb its power into your body. As you breathe in, you're drawing the Moon's light inwards, and as you exhale, imagine its light filling your body.
- I'd recommend moonbathing for twenty to forty minutes.
- When you're ready to finish, slowly become aware of your physical surroundings. Start to wiggle your fingers and toes, take a stretch and give yourself time to become fully present in the moment.
- Before you start doing something else, take some time to journal about your experience and/or pull an oracle or Tarot card.

You can moonbathe with all of the Moon phases to channel their distinctive energy.

If you keep finding yourself doing everything except what you should be doing, hello, procrastination, old friend! Treat yourself to a date with the waxing Moon to help boost your focus and motivation.

If you're calling in more abundance and opportunities, the full Moon may support you to manifest more of the good stuff.

If you're being a bit of a control freak and struggling to loosen your grip on an outcome, or perhaps resisting letting go of someone/something from the past, schedule in some time to a waning or new Moon to create space for something that will support you.

Or make moonbathing a nightly ritual to soak up all of the medicine that the Moon has to offer.

HOW TO CREATE YOUR OWN MOON CEREMONY

You can do this solo or gather your coven.

You will need:

- Candles
- Dried herbs (choose from those listed on page 147) or incense blend
- Charcoal disc, heated
- Heatproof dish
- Small pair of tongs
- Tarot or oracle cards
- Journal and pen
- Flowers
- Crystals and/or seashells
- Music

Preparation

Clean and tidy the space where you'll be doing the ceremony, making sure there isn't any clutter. Have a shower or bath so that you're feeling fresh, especially if you've just got back from a long day at work. Wear something comfortable, which makes you feel amazing. This doesn't include your favourite slouchy joggers with the holes in them or an overstretched hoody. Think of this as a date with the Moon!

Smoke-reset (see page 149) the area or room where you'll be

holding the ceremony and the altar space. Open the windows to release any unwanted energy. Add a pinch of dried herbs to the hot charcoal disc and walk along the edges of the room or circle the designated area, clockwise. Allow the smoke to drift through the air, purifying and blessing the space. You can use the smoke to cleanse yourself and your friends before you begin the ceremony.

Choose some relaxing, ambient music to have playing in the background. Light some candles and incense or diffuse an essential oil in an oil burner. Dim the lights.

It's likely you'll want to capture the experience on your phone, whether it's just for yourself or to share on social media, but we all know how distracting phones can be. You could either take some pictures before you begin or after you've finished. I'd recommend switching your phone either off or to flight mode for the ceremony. Put it in another room if it helps.

Create an altar (see page 224)
Creating an altar is a way of setting an intention for the ceremony. Consider what you would like to experience or activate. You can choose items and colours that represent a theme. See the new and full Moons (pages 55–79) for corresponding themes and crystals. Place on the altar items that act as a talisman for what you would like to manifest, or something you would like to charge with the supportive energy of the ceremony, or an offering to the Moon.

If you're solo doing a ceremony, I'd recommend placing the altar where you can sit in front of it. If you're doing this in a group, you could have it in the centre so that everyone can sit around it in a circle or set it up on a coffee table or mantelpiece.

The Ceremony

Opening

To open the ceremony, you could light a candle on the altar. You could bring your hands together in the prayer position, close your eyes and have a few moments' silence. You could chant 'Om' three times. You could read a poem. You could say your intention aloud. You could ring a bell or play a Tibetan or crystal singing bowl, if you have one.

If you're doing this in a group, you could discuss the themes of the Moon and what it's been illuminating or triggering for you all.

Meditate

Follow one of the Moon phase meditations (see page 257), according to the phase.

Meditation can help you tune out of your everyday distractions and get you into a calm headspace for the ceremony. If you have your own meditation practice, you could refer to that. Alternatively, you could listen to a guided meditation or chant mantras, courtesy of the internet. Check out YouTube, Spotify or meditation apps to find something that resonates with you. There are some really good free meditation apps (some have premium features if you subscribe). I recommend Insight Timer, which has a library of meditations. Chakra balancing, Moon, yoga nidra, meet your spirit guides, crystal singing bowls, chanting, relaxation, heart opening, manifestation, breathwork: you name it and someone will have recorded something soothing to take you on a meditative journey.

Choose a meditation to support you to align with the theme of the Moon you're working with.

Tarot spread
Working with Tarot or oracle cards is a great way to tune in and find out what the Moon is saying for you. You may have read some astrologers' interpretations of what's happening above us but don't forget that this is only a snapshot of what's going on in your situation. You'll find a series of card layouts (see pages 165–169) that will guide you to dive deeper and discover what the Moon is illuminating for you.

Ritual
See Moon Rituals (pages 215–256): take your pick.

Journalling
Spend some time writing about the illuminations, insights, epiphanies, triggers, resolutions and ideas that come to your attention during the ceremony. During such experiences you may feel as if you're in a bubble, but as soon as you step back into the 'real' world, the magic can fade pretty fast. It's like when you have a vivid dream that you forget by lunchtime. Journalling about your experience gives any little lightning bolts of truth somewhere to land and take root. You could also think of it as writing a note to your future self:

a reminder of a juicy truth bomb, proof that your intuition knew what it was talking about and a marker to a catalyst in your life.

Close

It's important to close the ceremony in a way that makes you feel protected and supported. This can help you integrate anything that comes from the experience. You could think of it as sealing the magic. It may help you feel more grounded when you resume your usual routine. To close, you could reflect on something you're grateful for. You could simply blow out the candle. You could ring a bell or play a Tibetan or crystal singing bowl, if you have one. If you've chanted 'Om' to open the ceremony, then chant it three times to close.

LUNAR GODDESSES AND GODS

Many cultures throughout history have revered gods and goddesses associated with the Moon – some were portrayed as the Moon itself. According to pagan and Wiccan traditions, you can call on one of these deities for guidance and support as you connect with the Moon.

ARTEMIS
Culture: Greek

Known as the goddess of the hunt, and also of the wilderness, wild animals, virginity and birth. Often depicted as a huntress with a bow and arrow. Protector of young children and assistant to women in childbirth. She is a maiden goddess, symbolized by the crescent Moon. Greek counterpart of Diana (see overleaf).

CERRIDWEN
Culture: Celtic

Known as the patron goddess of witches and wizards, Cerridwen is associated with the Moon, science, prophecy, poetry and fertility. Her name is taken from the Celtic word *cerru*, meaning cauldron. Cerridwen and the cauldron are associated with transformation, power, creative inspiration, wisdom, magic and rebirth. She is a crone goddess, symbolized by the waning Moon.

CHANDRA
Culture: Hindu

This Moon god is said to ride across the sky (at night) on a chariot pulled by ten white horses. Chandra is also known as Soma, which is the sap of plants. As he rides through the night, dew would form and people said that the plants were receiving life force from the Moon. Chandra is a fertility god: couples who struggle to conceive pray to him.

DIANA
Culture: Roman

Known as the goddess of the hunt and associated with nature and animals. Diana is also thought of as a fertility goddess, and women who want to conceive or have a safe and easy labour worship her. She took on the role as goddess of the Moon after Luna. Roman counterpart of Artemis (see page 203).

HEKATE (HECATE)
Culture: Greek

Known as the goddess of witchcraft, magic, the Moon, night, ghosts and communicating with the dead. She is also said to be a goddess of crossroads and a gatekeeper between worlds. Hekate is often depicted holding two torches, which are symbolic of her wisdom. She may be called upon for protection. Often accompanied by two animal familiars. She is a crone goddess, associated with the waning and dark Moon.

ISIS
Culture: Egyptian

Known as a fertility goddess as well as a goddess of magic and healing. Said to be one of the most powerful goddesses. She protects women and children, and is associated with motherhood. It was believed that she can heal the sick, and is associated with rebirth because she brought Osiris (her brother) back to life for one night. Isis is a Moon and Sun deity.

IX CHEL
Culture: Mayan

Known as a goddess of the Moon and associated with fertility and childbirth. The ancient Mayans said that Ix Chel would wander the sky, and when she couldn't be seen, she would be in a cenote (a natural underground water reservoir). She is the Sun's lover. This goddess has two aspects: a youthful and sensual woman, and a wise, powerful aged woman, the crone. Mayanists debate if they might actually be two individual goddesses.

KHONSU
Culture: Egyptian

Khonsu is an Ancient Egyptian god; his name means the Traveller or the Wanderer, which relates to his journeys across the night sky. Khonsu is said to be a fierce defender against evil spirits and he can be invoked for protection. He is also worshipped as a god of love and fertility, likened to a virile bull. He is associated with the crescent Moon.

KUAN YIN
Culture: Chinese

Known as a goddess of compassion, kindness and mercy, Kuan Yin is associated with Buddhism as a Bodhisattva and

also has a male form because representations of Bodhisattva
are masculine. She is also depicted with many arms, and varying numbers of eyes, heads and hands. This was a symbol of
her omnipresence: she is able to see or reach out to anyone
in need. Kuan Yin is a mother-goddess and is said to relieve
suffering.

LUNA
Culture: Roman

Luna is the embodiment of the Moon – she *is* the Moon,
according to ancient Roman history. This goddess is the
divine feminine to complement Sol (the Sun God). Luna is
associated with the cycles of life and the tides of the ocean.
Often invoked for her intuitive power, femininity, creativity, blessings, her alignment with the element of water, protection and safety in travel. Roman counterpart to Selene
(see below).

SELENE
Culture: Greek

Selene is the Titan goddess of the Moon, which she person-
ifies, according to Ancient Greeks. It's said that she drives
her chariot across the night sky, powered by white horses.
She governs the lunar cycles and is traditionally worshipped
on the new and full Moon. Selene is a patron goddess of
femininity, said to inspire love, and has the power to ease

childbirth. Her powers are also associated with awakening intuition, dreams and psychic visions. Greek counterpart to Luna (see page 209).

YEMANJA
Culture: African and Native South American

Known as a major water deity, Yemanja is a powerful goddess of the oceans. She is often depicted as a mermaid and represents the ebb and flow of life, just like the ocean flows. Yemanja is associated with motherhood and protection. She brings life but can also cause destruction, as a catalyst for change. This goddess invites us to surrender and embrace the cycles of life. She is symbolized by the waxing crescent Moon.

*

Invocation

To call upon one of these deities for a Moon ritual or ceremony, you can place a picture, oracle card, talisman or figurine that represents your chosen god or goddess on your altar. If you're using a talisman or figurine, you can consecrate it for your altar by placing it somewhere safe outside or on a windowsill during a full Moon to absorb the energy of the Moon's light overnight before use.

The Hotline

When you place your deity's representation on your altar, sit in front of them with your eyes closed and your hands resting in your lap, palms facing up; this signifies being open to receive. Take a few slow, deep breaths, to allow you to connect and feel present in the moment. Call the deity into the space by saying, 'I invite <insert deity> to guide, teach, protect, heal and bless me. May I feel, understand and express your power and wisdom. For the good of our Planet Earth and all living beings upon it.' You may want to visualize them stepping forward, if that feels appropriate for you. Spend a few minutes in silence to support the connection you have created with your deity. If you have Tarot or oracle cards, you could pull a card and ask: 'What does <insert deity name> want me to know?' I'd recommend placing an offering in front of the representation of your deity. This could be money, flower petals, dried rice (uncooked), seeds or nuts as a gesture of gratitude to them. Then bring your hands into the prayer position.

Take a deep breath. Carry out your Moon ritual or ceremony when you are ready.

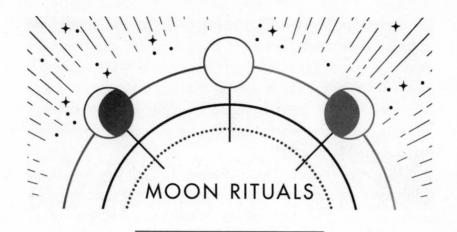

MOON RITUALS

You could think of a ritual as an active meditation, creating space to tune in and align with the Moon and get grounded. An opportunity to be 100 per cent present in the here and now. When you slow down enough, you can turn up the volume to your intuition and become ultra-clear on what's coming up for you and how you want to move forward. Call it self-care, healing, reclamation, empowerment, it's all sacred time that you'll thank yourself for.

GETTING STARTED

You don't have to be in a coven to practise any of this. All you need to do is find a place that feels safe, where you won't be disturbed, at home or among nature. I'd recommend designating somewhere to do your rituals because the energy can build there. It's like creating a personal temple (see Sacred Space, page 17). You can perform your rituals solo or gather some friends or loved ones to create your own ceremony. If you can't get everyone together, why not arrange a group Skype or FaceTime date so that you can meet up virtually, wherever you are in the world? I've led Moon ceremonies on Instagram Live, where hundreds of people have joined to make some Moon magic.

It can be overwhelming (hands up, I've felt that way, too), thinking you need to do everything at the right time to get in on the good stuff. Note that when it comes to new and full Moons, their energy can be felt up to two days before and after the peak of their transition so you have a reasonable window in which to do something. Some people find it too intense when the Moon peaks at these times so they hold out until things have settled before doing any rituals. So, don't panic when you see people on social media talking about the Moon tonight and you've already made plans or couldn't get tickets to a Moon ceremony. The hype can make you feel like you missed the memo for a must-see gig. This isn't a Black Friday sale: the Moon isn't going anywhere.

I want to emphasize that you don't have to do everything I share in this book and follow it to a T to lock down the life of your dreams. On some new and full Moons I don't do anything except some of my daily rituals (see page 121) and perhaps pull a Tarot or oracle card. You don't have to have an altar or a crystal grid, or even own Tarot cards, unless you want to. When I'm holding Moon ceremonies or I plan to be ultra-intentional with something I'd like to manifest, then I love to be extra with all of this. I'll use flowers, crystals, incense, candles, cauldron and rituals *but* the frills don't necessarily give the ceremony any extra power. All of this can help you drop deeper into a meditative state to align with the energies you're calling in, but it's the intention that activates it all. Some of my juiciest 'wins' have come through quickie rituals. Like, writing my unlimited day in the notes app on my phone while I was on a flight to Croatia. Or creating a sigil (see page 217) in my notebook while I was sitting on the train to London. There are times when less is more, which is why I'm including some practices that you can do on your phone without any paraphernalia: we're all aware of how life can get in the way of our plans.

Sometimes you'll want to do one of these rituals when the current Moon phase doesn't correspond and you'll feel called to do your own thing. Go for it. Trust what your intuition is saying. You do you. Doing these rituals at the specific lunations can call in some back-up from the universe but don't feel you have to wait until the Moon is 'right' for you to do what needs to be done. If you've finally had enough of your ex toying with your emotions and the Moon is waxing, you needn't wait until it wanes to do a cord-cutting ritual (see page 246). If you've had an idea you can't stop thinking about, you needn't wait until the new or full Moon to set your intentions for it. These rituals are all adaptable so don't be restricted by the specific Moon phases: you could do the altar (page 224) and bath (page 242) rituals to celebrate the solstices and equinoxes. Try the space-clearing ritual (page 248) on New Year's Day or when you move into a new home. You can do the vision board (page 221) for your birthday to tune into what you'd like to manifest during your next trip around the Sun. When you do these rituals you are making a commitment to yourself. Follow them according to what you need at the time, not just when the Moon says so.

Every moment of every day is an opportunity to make your own magic.

Before you perform any of these rituals, read through the steps at least once so that you can familiarize yourself with what has to be done and to make sure you have everything you need to get the most out of the experience. The rituals are a starting point for you: develop what feels right for you. Get creative, add things, leave things out and, most importantly, use the rituals to get to know your intuition on a deeper level.

NEW MOON
Good things are coming

A new Moon is like a permission slip to start fresh. Working with this phase of the Moon can support you in slowing down and reflecting on how you'd like to move forward. Think of it as a time to say a huge 'Yes' to making some overdue changes in your life.

Sigil Ritual

A sigil is a symbol that represents an intention. You could think of it as a logo for something you'd like to manifest. You take a specific intention, phrase or affirmation and use the letters to transform it into a symbol. It can be a powerful practice that you use to reprogramme limiting beliefs that are holding you back. It's said that our thoughts create our reality: maybe you've been complaining about something more than you'd like to admit, or an internal dialogue is holding you back from breaking a cycle that you're oh-so-ready for.

Think of your words as a spell. Take notice of what you're saying and check that it's conjuring the outcome you *really* want.

You will need:

- A charcoal disc
- A small pair of tongs
- A lighter or matches
- Heatproof bowl or cauldron
- Dried mint, rose or rosemary, or incense
- Alternative option for suggested herbs: White Sage, Palo Santo or sweetgrass, if you have it, but please read page 150 on sustainability
- Pen and paper – to design and practise your sigil
- A crystal or item to inscribe with your sigil (optional)
- A Sharpie or permanent marker (I love metallic inks for this)

What to do:

- Hold the charcoal disc with the tongs and light the edge of the charcoal with a match or lighter. Once it's ignited, immediately place it in the heatproof dish. Wait until the charcoal is glowing entirely before adding a sprinkle of your dried herbs or incense. Add a small pinch at a time. In this case, less is better.
- Allow the smoke (see smoke-reset ritual, page 149) to wash over you and reset your aura. Imagine it transforming any unwanted energy or distractions as it washes over you.
- Hold the item you're going to inscribe with the sigil over the smoke at a safe distance to cleanse it (energetically).

Visualize yourself surrounded by white light or any colour that inspires you.

- Either sitting or lying down, close your eyes and take a few slow breaths in your own time.
- Then, take a deep breath into your belly and breathe out slowly. As you exhale, feel yourself landing fully in the here and now. Feel your body connected to the Earth or supported by the surface beneath you.
- Start by writing down your intention as a statement. I always recommend beginning the sentence in the present tense, as if it's already happening for you: 'I am', 'I'm open to' or 'It's safe for me.' For example:

'I am supported.'
'I'm open to a relationship where I am loved, passionate, inspired and respected.'
'Money flows to me easily.'
'It's safe for me to take this opportunity.'

- When you have your statement, begin to cross out the vowels and any repeating letters.

I A M S U P P O R T E D = M S R T D

- With a pen and paper, doodle with the remaining letters to design your sigil. You could try overlapping, reversing or rotating them, add other symbols, whatever feels good to you. Be creative. If it looks weird, you're doing it right, because it's supposed to look nothing like the original letters. This process allows your subconscious to receive the message of the symbol, while your conscious mind disconnects from the meaning behind it. Spend as long as you need until you've designed an image you're happy with and feel excited about. Memorize what it looks like.

- Then use the permanent marker to inscribe your chosen item with your sigil.
- Once it's drawn, close your eyes and visualize the symbol in your mind. Imagine the sigil infusing into the item and say your statement aloud three times.

- If you've drawn your sigil on a piece of paper, you can burn it somewhere safe, or if you've chosen a candle for this, light the candle.
- If you've inscribed it on a crystal, you can either keep it close by or bury it somewhere in the earth. Trust that this is the beginning of something wonderful opening up for you. You could either spend some time meditating or journalling, or simply enjoy a cup of your favourite herbal tea infusion, to give this new intention some space to integrate with your consciousness.

The Vision Board

A vision board is a visual representation of what you'd like to manifest in your life, often created with magazine cuttings and photographs. The idea is that you keep it somewhere you will see it regularly to remind you of what you're calling in and nudge you to make decisions that will support your intention. You could keep it by your desk, on your fridge, in your bedroom, on your altar, wherever you like. Another option is to put it somewhere safe that you *won't* see it, like under your bed, as if you were sowing a seed and you're trusting that it's taken root but you can come back and reflect on it later to see if anything needs changing or updating and, most excitingly, if any of it has come to fruition.

You can either do this old-school by creating a physical collage of images and words that relate to what you'd like to activate in your life or create a Pinterest board and 'pin' images to it that relate in the same way.

You will need:

- A selection of pens and pencils
- Magazines
- A piece of canvas or cardboard
- Scissors
- Glue or washi tape (a type of sticky tape)

What to do:

- Write your intention on the centre of your canvas or cardboard, then begin selecting images and words from magazines that inspire and represent what you'd like to manifest. Use these words and images to express yourself and dream big.
- Mindfully arrange and stick your cut-outs on to your canvas or cardboard to create your vision board.
- Look out for any themes from your subconscious that are being communicated through your board. Take some time to reflect and write in your journal about any insights or ideas that have come to you from doing this ritual.

Pinterest Vision Board
You will need:

- A digital device: smartphone, tablet, laptop or PC
- A Pinterest account and app installed

What to do:

- Create a new Pinterest board (instructions on the website, if you're new to how it works); set it to secret if you don't want it to be visible to anyone else.
- Title the board with either the Moon phase and zodiac sign that it's in or with your new Moon intention.
- Type your keywords into the search bar or check out some of your favourite accounts for inspiration. You could look out for quotes, pictures of interiors, landscapes, activities, people, destinations, locations, clothing, jewellery, tools or technology. When you see an image that may associate with your new Moon intention and what you'd like to manifest, pin it to your board.
- Keep pinning images that you like and arrange them on your board in a way that feels aesthetically pleasing to you.
- Look out for any themes from your subconscious that are being communicated through your Pinterest vision board. Take some time to reflect and write in your journal about any insights or ideas that come to you from doing this ritual.

MOON ALTAR

An altar is a space to focus your intentions. You could think of it as a three-dimensional vision board (see page 221). Creating an altar can be a mindful practice where you choose items that have a meaning for you. It's a reflection of what you're calling in and the things that inspire and support you, including mementos of what you're grateful for and happy times. You can dedicate a corner of your home, a bedside table, a shelf, a desk, a fireplace or a windowsill to your altar, anywhere you like as long as it won't be disturbed and you can either sit in front of it or see it frequently. It can be a permanent fixture or something you create each time you do a Moon ritual, celebrate a solstice or an equinox or whenever you feel called to.

You can use crystals, flowers, plants, photos, shells, Tarot or oracle cards, trinkets and talismans, heirlooms, inspiring quotes or poetry, figurines, images of deities, candles, anything that's significant to the life you're living and weaving. It can be simple and minimalist or extra and maximalist. Small or big. You get to choose. There isn't a right or wrong way to create an altar as long as it's meaningful to you.

Traditional Wiccan altars have an athame (a ceremonial blade or knife), a chalice, a pentacle, a wand, a cauldron, a broom, candles and incense. Each item has a specific significance and is a tool to focus and direct spiritual/psychic energy.

Always keep your altar clean, tidy and uncluttered. Treat this sacred space as if it is sacred.

You will need:

- Items for your altar (see suggestions above)

What to do:

- What would you like your altar to symbolize? How do you want to feel when you're in front of it? Choose items based on your answers to these questions. Note: you don't need to go on an internet shopping spree to source pieces for your altar. You can use items you already have or forage for seasonal gifts from Mother Nature. I'd recommend getting new candles but it doesn't have to look Instagram-worthy.
- Prepare the designated area and make sure it's clean and clutter-free. You can energetically cleanse the space and altar items using smoke from dried herbs (see page 149).
- Mindfully place each item on your altar. Take your time to arrange things until they feel as if they're where they need to be. It can be simple, symmetrical, flamboyant, understated, overstated, colourful or monochrome. Express yourself and your intentions through your altar.
- When you've finished putting it all together, sit back and take some time to connect with the altar in front of you.

You could simply sit in front of it and meditate there (page 122). You could take a slow, nourishing deep breath, and as you exhale, imagine that you're breathing life into the altar to activate it. You could pull a Tarot or oracle card and ask: what will support me to stay connected with this intention? Do whatever feels good for you, before rushing to take a picture of it for social media.

As always, these suggestions are adaptable and you're encouraged to create your altar in a way you feel intuitively guided to.

Real Life It

If you don't have time to do a new Moon ritual, treat the day as if it were a living ritual.

Consider that today is the first day of a new phase in your life: what would you do? New Moons are all about beginnings and can support new habits or regimens. Starting a practice on a new Moon is said to gain extra traction as the energy of the Moon builds. Think of the Moon as your running buddy. You don't need any witchy paraphernalia for this one, just to start walking your talk. What have you been putting off until now? What do you keep saying you don't have time for? Use the new Moon to start as you mean to go on.

WAXING MOON
Energy flows where attention goes

You've set those new Moon intentions and now it's time to do something about them. Work with the waxing Moon to get things moving in the right direction. This is the ideal time to create a strategy, get prepared and be proactive so that you can cultivate something sustainable.

Less Talk, More Action

If you could do one thing each day towards your new Moon intention, what would those actions be? Work back from the goal and ask yourself: what can I do today, this week and next month that will support it to become reality? Work out how long each task will take and schedule the actions in your diary. For a longer task, you could allocate yourself an amount of time to work on it each day. Give yourself one task per day: it's less overwhelming and more likely to happen. I'd recommend doing your task first thing in the morning so that it's a priority and less likely to be met with the excuse that you didn't have time. Otherwise, work out a time that suits your schedule better. Here are some examples of tasks:

• • • POSSIBLE ACTIONS • • •

- Revamping your CV
- Signing up to a dating app
- Meditating
- Buying a domain name for a new venture
- Pulling a daily oracle card
- Booking an appointment with your doctor or dentist
- Enrolling on a course
- Buying a book
- Opening a bank account
- Researching travel destinations
- Watching a documentary
- Going to a protest
- Applying for a new job or attending a networking event
- Having a consultation with a life coach
- Doing your laundry
- Batch-cooking nourishing food that you can store in the freezer
- Practising yoga
- Having time off
- Exercising

Accountability Buddies

A little bit of accountability can go a long way to make sure that you do what you say you will. Do this with your friend, partner, children or best witches so that you can support and cheer each other on. In the morning, message your accountability buddy/ies to let them know three things: (a) What you're grateful for, (b) What you're going to achieve today/ this week/this Moon cycle, and (c) What you're excited about. Share whatever feels true for you. I really like WhatsApp for this because you can use it to leave short and sweet voice messages for each other.

You can do this on the waxing Moon or make it a morning ritual where you send each other messages: it doesn't have to be every day. It could be from Monday to Friday so that you've got the weekend to rest and recharge, which are both actions too.

Waxing Moon Soundtrack

Music is so emotive and can help you get in the right frame of mind to slay. Create a playlist of songs related to your new Moon intention.

If you're calling in more money or clients, curate songs focused on money and success. If you're cultivating more confidence, line up songs that make you feel like you're winning. If you're calling in love, find songs that get you in the mood. If you're calling in support for a challenging situation at work, choose songs that help you feel supported. If you're calling in peace of mind, think Ibiza chill-out vibes.

You could create your playlist on the waxing Moon: listen to it in the morning, when you're on your way to work, when you're going through your to-do list, while you're exercising or as you're getting ready for bed.

FULL MOON
Gratitude is my attitude

Full Moons are a time for illumination and a culmination of the seeds that were sown since the corresponding new Moon (which happened six months earlier). Even if things didn't work out as you had anticipated, celebrate your wins, big or small. You could work with the full Moon to revaluate and adjust (if necessary) the intentions you set during the new Moon. This is an abundant time and you can use the Moon phase to attract more of the good stuff.

Love Spell

The intention of this love spell is for you to soak up some warm fuzzy feelings (with a dose of crystal healing), get clear on what you need and *be* the love that you wish to receive and experience. Single, loved up or somewhere in between, this one's for you.

We are much more magnetic when we already feel as if we've got what we need and aren't expecting someone or something to complete us. When our hearts are open, it's easier to embrace the good things in life. It doesn't matter how much someone adores you if you aren't feeling it yourself.

If you're single this could result in you either not going through with a date because you subconsciously think you're not good enough for them, or you keep going on regretful dates. If you're in a relationship, this can result in a rocky patch when you wonder where the love has gone. If you're craving more love in your life but keep repeating the same patterns, it's time to look in the mirror (not literally).

For example, if you keep attracting lovers who are emotionally unavailable, in what ways are you being emotionally unavailable to yourself? Or maybe you have a haunting sense that you're destined to be single for ever, which isn't helped by Susan asking, 'Why are you still single, when you're such a catch?'

'I wish I knew,' you reply, through gritted teeth and a forced smile.

Take some time to reflect on your traumas and heartbreak. Are any fears about being in a relationship lurking in the shadows? If you're in a relationship, which of your needs are not being met, and how are you catering for your own needs among everyone else's? If anything comes to mind, this is where the healing work needs to be focused.

You will need:

- A pink or rose-scented candle
- A pen and paper
- Two pieces of rose quartz
- A drawstring pouch (optional)
- 1–3 additional crystals for love

• • • CRYSTALS FOR LOVE • • •

Rose quartz can support forgiveness, acceptance and unconditional love

Kunzite can help you check out of Heartbreak Hotel and start trusting that history doesn't have to repeat itself (again)

Garnet represents empowerment, courage, sensuality and, most of all, commitment

Danburite can support you to attract like-minded people

Aquamarine can help you to reprogramme outdated thought processes and attachments

Cobalto calcite can remind you of how sexy you are and enhance sensuality

Tip: when choosing a crystal for this love spell, it doesn't have to be from this list. If you're at a crystal shop ask yourself, 'Which crystal will support me to open up to love?' and see which you're drawn to. If you have a copy of *The Crystal Code* hold the book in your hand, close your eyes and ask, 'Which crystal will support me to open up to love?' then open the book at random to see which crystal chooses you.

What to do:

- On the night before or on the full Moon, choose the crystals that represent what you'd like to experience and, with the two pieces of rose quartz, cleanse them by holding the crystals under a tap of running water for a minute. Imagine any unwanted energy being washed away.
- Then leave the crystals to be charged by the Moon's light either outside (somewhere safe) or on a windowsill. You can leave the crystals to charge for a few hours or overnight.
- The next day, create a sacred space (see page 17). Tidy your bedroom and put fresh sheets on your bed.
- Light the candle and say, 'Let the love in.'
- Write a list of words that express how you'd like to feel in your relationship, the qualities and values the other person would ideally have, things you might have in common, mutual goals, and what you'd like to experience with that person. You could reflect on previous relationships to get clear on what's non-negotiable, or remember when you first met your partner and you were in the honeymoon phase to remind you of what's possible.
- Write this statement and fill in the gaps, 'If it's for the highest good of all, I'm open to a relationship where I feel _____ and we can both be_____. I'd love it if we _____ together. I'm calling in this or something better so that we can all rise together.'
- The two pieces of rose quartz represent you and your partner, and the other crystals represent themes to support

you. Hold the crystals to your heart and say your statement aloud to programme and activate them.

• Sleep with the love-spell crystals in your bed. You can keep them in a drawstring pouch if you want to make sure they stay together in one place and you avoid waking up in the middle of the night because there's a crystal digging into your side.

Gratitude List

Get your journal, or use the notes app on your smartphone, and write 100 things you are grateful for. It may seem challenging but stick with it. See page 138 for the benefits of gratitude.

CHARGE YOUR CRYSTALS

Is it even a full Moon if someone isn't reminding you on Instagram to charge your crystals? I love seeing these posts, knowing that people all over the world are putting their crystal babies out to soak up some moonbeams. Crystals and minerals come from the Earth: they always appreciate a dose of vitamin moonlight and reconnecting with nature. Like plugging in your phone to charge, you're plugging your crystals into nature to give them a boost.

Leave your crystals in the garden or on a windowsill overnight to reset and recharge during the full Moon. You don't have to do this with all of your crystals for every full Moon. You could choose a particular Moon, like full Moon in Pisces if you'd like to be infused with some dreamy and intuitive lunar energies, or full Moon in Aries, for a confidence and motivation boost.

Put your crystals out to charge as a practice in mindfulness. Take your time and keep it intentional. Focus on placing each crystal as if you were plugging it into the Moon. Sit with them in meditation for a while after you've put them down to charge.

PROSPERITY CRYSTAL GRID

Tap into the abundant energy of the full Moon with a crystal grid. Crystals can support us with our intentions and Moon wishes; when used to create a grid the energy may be amplified. This ritual may help you focus on and activate your intention.

You will need:

- A charcoal disc
- Heatproof bowl or cauldron
- A lighter or matches
- Your journal and a pen
- A banknote
- 4 clear quartz points
- A crystal of your choice for the centre of the grid

- 4–12 crystals of your choice to surround the central crystal
- A crystal wand, large crystal point or selenite wand to activate the grid
- Cinnamon, dried powder or crushed bark
- Candles (optional)

What to do:

- Set up a sacred space. Perhaps light some candles and a charcoal disc in the heatproof bowl so that it's ready for when you need it.
- In your journal, write a list of the things you'd like to be able to pay for over the next month. This may include your bills, debts, holidays or spending money, education, personal development, healing treatments, clothes, food and savings, whatever you need money for. Write down each item with the amount it will cost next to it. Then add up the total sum. Write: 'I'm open to manifesting [insert amount], as long as it serves the highest good of all.'
- Place the banknote in the centre of where you're going to create the grid.
- Hold your central crystal in your left hand and say, 'Money flows to me,' three times, then place the crystal on top of the banknote.
- Lay four clear quartz points around the central crystal. Place them in the directions of north, east, south and west, with the points facing outwards.
- Place the other crystals around the central crystal to create a symmetrical pattern.

• • • CRYSTALS FOR ABUNDANCE • • •

Citrine can give you the confidence to create or say yes to opportunities

Pyrite can enhance your self-worth and magnetism

Amazonite can support new businesses and ventures

Green aventurine can support you to cultivate a better relationship with money

Cheetah jasper can help to align you with being in the right place at the right time

Clear quartz can help you focus, clear limiting beliefs and amplify your intention

- Using the crystal wand, touch the crystal in the centre, then touch each crystal surrounding the main crystal, going in a clockwise direction. Do this as if you were connecting the dots until you complete a circle.
- Sprinkle a pinch of cinnamon over the preheated charcoal disc and allow the smoke to wash over the grid to bless it. Cinnamon is used for cleansing (energetic) and attracting prosperity and abundance.
- Spend some time meditating with your activated crystal grid.
- Express gratitude for the abundance you already have in your life and the potential of what's coming.

Sleep Ritual

A study by Professor Christian Cajochen and his team at Basel University has shown that the full Moon may affect our sleep. It's said that volunteers spent 30 per cent less time in deep sleep and slept on average twenty minutes less than usual. Perhaps full Moon insomnia isn't a mystical myth. If you find it hard to sleep in the nights surrounding the full Moon, or any other for that matter, this ritual will help you drift into a night of deep sleep.

Lavender essential oil is famous for its calming effects and rose essential oil is also nurturing and balancing. They're both healing plants that can soothe anxiety and guide you to unplug from the outside world and any frenetic thoughts. Lepidolite, rose quartz and selenite are soothing and harmonizing, and black tourmaline is protective and grounding. The combination of these crystals can help you feel supported and as if you're being tucked up safely in bed. Their energies can anchor you in a relaxed state. I'd suggest placing either the lepidolite, selenite or rose quartz on your forehead as it aligns with your third eye. Putting a crystal here can help to quieten the mind. Placing the black tourmaline below the navel can bring energy to the lower part of the body, which may help you to feel more grounded and supported.

You will need:

- Lavender room spray (substitute with rose or palma rose, if pregnant)
- A small piece of lepidolite, selenite or rose quartz, and black tourmaline

What to do:

- Perform a smoke-reset ritual (see page 149).
- Spray the lavender room spray in your bedroom and over your bed.
- Nothing beats sleeping in fresh bed linen so if you're up for being 'extra', get them on! You'll thank yourself afterwards. Put on your favourite PJs and get ready to unwind.
- Lie on your bed and get comfortable.
- Place a piece of lepidolite, selenite or rose quartz on your forehead. Place a piece of black tourmaline just beneath your navel.
- Close your eyes and bring your awareness to your breathing, simply watching the natural movement of your breath

as it flows in and out of your body. Scan your body and sense each part relaxing.

- Imagine the colours of the crystals infusing your body and visualize the energy of the crystals being absorbed.
- Take a slow, deep breath into your body. Imagine the presence of the Earth rising up to meet your body, and as you exhale, feel yourself relaxing deeply into the bed.

Stay like this for as long as you want to. Remove the crystals when you're ready and get in position to sleep, so that you can drift into a night of sweet dreams.

Abundance Bath Ritual

Make like a goddess and treat yourself to some opulence with a ritual bath. You can be as extra as you like: use your favourite beauty products and surround yourself with things that make you feel lavish. Fresh towels and clean sheets to slide into afterwards are a must.

You will need:

- Candles and incense
- 300g Epsom, Himalayan or Dead Sea salt
- Roses or other flowers
- 4 tumbled moonstones
- 1 clear quartz point
- Additional crystals (suggestions: moonstone, smoky quartz, amethyst, rose quartz or clear quartz)
- Seashells

- See also suggested crystal recommendations for the corresponding full Moon according to its zodiac alignment (pages 55–79)

What to do:

- Light some candles and incense in the bathroom.
- Place a tumbled moonstone in each corner of the bath rim.
- Place any additional crystals on the sides of the bath rim, in the centre.
- Place the clear quartz point in the bath.
- Add 300g of natural salt to the bath.
- Fill the bath with warm water, ensuring that it's a comfortable temperature and depth.
- Before getting in, scatter rose petals on the water. As you pick up each petal, think of something you're grateful for.
- Relax in the bath for at least twenty minutes or as long as you like. Imagine that you're bathing in love, support and abundance.
- When you're ready to finish, remove the crystals and flowers before you pull out the plug. Don't rush to get out: wait until all of the water has drained away. Visualize any distractions being drawn away from you as the water is released.

If you don't have a bath:

- Light some candles and incense in the bathroom.
- Place a tumbled moonstone in each corner of the shower tray.

- Place a clear quartz or amethyst on the sides of the shower tray, in the centre.
- As if you were turning your shower into an altar, put roses on the shower unit. Tuck flowers behind your toiletries and wherever they'll fit without causing any damage. As you place each flower, think of something you're grateful for.
- Relax under the shower, and as the water washes over you, imagine that you're being bathed in love, support and abundance.
- When you're ready to get out, turn off the water and use your hand to wipe over yourself in a sweeping motion. Visualize brushing any distractions away from your body and aura.

Upgrade You

One of the themes of a full Moon is abundance, and it's a potent time to implement upgrades in your life to symbolize that you're moving onwards and upwards.

Upgrade suggestions:

- Throw away old underwear and socks with holes. Treat yourself to new.
- Set up a monthly direct debit to a charity you'd like to support.
- Buy a new wallet.
- Invest in a reusable cup for your takeaway drinks.
- Upgrade your phone.

- Hire a personal/virtual assistant.
- Sign up to a course or meet with someone who can support you to take things to the next level.
- Invest in something for your business or hobby.
- Invest in therapy or sessions with a healer.
- Schedule days with your family and friends, if you've been working too much.
- Book a holiday.
- Say no to an outdated obligation.
- Marie Kondo your home.
- Open a savings account.

Your upgrade shouldn't put you in debt: we're not here to fake it until we make it. Keep it real. Choose something that makes your life easier, gives something back, makes you feel amazing and/or feeds your soul. If there's something you keep moaning about, use that to inspire what you upgrade. If some of these suggestions seem unrealistic for you, what could be your first step towards an upgrade in the future? That step is your first upgrade. Incremental expansions can help you feel as if you're closer to the ultimate goal. No upgrade is too small.

WANING MOON
Let it hurt then let it go

The waning Moon is the time to weed out anything that isn't working for you, such as any limiting beliefs, relationships or situations. Work with this Moon phase to declutter and create space for more of what you truly want.

Cord-cutting Ritual

If you've been trying to move forward but someone or something keeps dragging you back, this ritual may help you release yourself from the attachment. It can be used for cutting the cord and letting go of an ex, a frenemy, situations from your past, comparisons, limiting beliefs or behaviours, so that you can feel lighter and be free.

You need to do this ritual only once for a specific situation; even if you don't notice immediate results, trust that the healing is in action. When we repeatedly do a cord-cutting ritual because we think it isn't working, we're actually reinforcing the belief that the connection is still there, which is the last thing you want if you're trying to detach. Trust the process.

You will need:

- A large crystal point (I recommend clear quartz, black obsidian or rose quartz)
- Rosemary or lavender essential oil

What to do:

- Create a sacred space (see page 17) and make sure you won't be disturbed.
- Sit comfortably, and close your eyes. Take three slow, deep breaths to support you to bring your attention to the present moment. Spend some time in silence: whenever your thoughts wander, observe your breath.
- Take some deep breaths, and as you breathe in, visualize yourself calling back your power from the person, situation or limiting belief. As you exhale send back the energy you've been holding on to that doesn't belong to you.
- When you feel embodied, say (aloud or in your mind), 'I forgive you. I release you so that we can be free.'
- Pick up the crystal and hold it in your left hand. Visualize the crystal being absorbed into your body – you could imagine white light moving in through your left hand, up your arm and filling you from the soles of your feet to the top of your head. Clear quartz represents new beginnings, clarity and purification, and it's replacing what you've just released. Soak up this energy for as long as you want to.
- When you feel as if you've taken what you need from the crystal, place it in front of you or on your altar.

- Drip one or two drops of rosemary or lavender essential oil into your hand. Rub your palms together, then hold them in front of your face and inhale deeply, breathing in the fragrance of the oil and exhaling slowly. Next, place your hands over your chest, inhale deeply and connect with your heart, then exhale slowly. Move your hands down and place them over your abdomen, just above your navel, inhale deeply and connect with your solar plexus chakra. Exhale slowly.
- Bring your hands to rest in your lap.
- Take one more slow, deep breath. Begin to move your body: rotate your neck, stretch your arms into the air, then wrap them around your body to give yourself a hug.
- When you're ready, open your eyes and reconnect with your surroundings.
- Before you carry on with your day, you could spend some time journalling or pull an oracle card for guidance.

Space-clearing Ritual

Think of the way that a fragrance can awaken your senses. Choose a candle that inspires you in some way. When you use candles in rituals, the flame ignites your intention and symbolizes transformation. It can be a simple act that opens you to new perspectives, experiences and opportunities. Decide which room to use to perform the ritual: it could be your bedroom if you're focusing on relationships and intimacy, your workspace for business goals, your bathroom or dressing-table for body positivity, wherever you feel called to make some magic happen.

You will need:

- A charcoal disc
- A small pair of tongs
- A lighter or matches
- Heatproof bowl or cauldron
- A candle: you can use any type, even a simple tealight. For special occasions, I like to treat myself to a candle that has a specific meaning behind it, or a scent that could add some power to my intention, like rose for love, lavender for calm, rosemary for focus, eucalyptus for new beginnings, or a smell that instantly reminds me of somewhere exotic
- Dried bay leaf, cardamom, mint or rosemary
- Alternative option for suggested herbs: White Sage, Palo Santo or sweetgrass, if you have it, but please read page 150 on sustainability
- A song that represents the energy you want to bring into your room

What to do:

- Begin by cleaning, decluttering and tidying your space.
- Dispose of any old candles from this area. If they can be recycled, then please do so. I always try to use up old candles before I do this so that they aren't wasted, or put them somewhere else to be used at another time. *Cleaning the*

space and removing the old candles represents creating space for a new beginning.

- If you have dried herbs, White Sage, Palo Santo or incense, you can use them to smoke-cleanse the area to reset the energy (see page 149). Open the windows and doors so that the energy you're casting out has an exit. You can also drift the smoke over your body to cleanse your energy. As you do this, say to yourself, 'I release any energy that doesn't serve me or belong here.'

- Light your candle and say to yourself, 'May this be a safe and sacred space filled with love/joy/inspiration/passion/creativity/trust/laughter/peace/harmony.'

- Choose your favourite song or a playlist that invokes the feelings you want for the space; press play and turn up the volume. Feel free to have a little dance.

If you're using a small candle, like a tealight, allow it to burn to the end, as long as it's safe to do so. When using a large candle, let it burn for as long as you want; each time you relight it, say your intention.

Social Media Detox

We're spending more and more time on social media, and the accounts that we follow can impact our mental health, whether we realize it or not. For example, if you scroll first thing in the morning, you have no control over what you're going to see and it can set the tone for your day ahead. The worst-case scenario is that you see something that's like a dagger through your heart or nails scraping down a chalkboard, and it puts you in a funk that you can't shake. Nobody wants that.

My friend Lucy Sheridan is a comparison coach and she talks about the 'House Party Rule' when it comes to who we follow (or don't) on social media. The criteria are:

If you wouldn't allow the person, brand or thing to come into your home or inner circle, then you should review whether or not they stay in your social media feed.

Would you invite them to your house party? Flood your feed with the things that nourish you, make you feel good, entertain you and challenge you in all the right ways.

It's not about creating echo chambers and wrapping ourselves in cotton wool. Although there will be times when we need to take extreme self-care and be very careful about the stimuli we're access- ing. If we're feeling steady with our mental health, though, social media can be a fantastic source of education and understanding of what's going on in the world.

Call back your power and curate a feed that aligns with your highest self. If you don't want to follow Karen down the road talking about her new eyelashes, it's cool. It isn't personal. We're all entitled to autonomy over who we sub- scribe to. Use this as an opportunity to cut ties with exes, past soul-sucking jobs and frenemies. Stop cyberstalking people who aren't in your life any more. This waning Moon ritual is simple and you could do it in your lunch break or while you're commuting on public transport.

You will need:

- Your phone
- A microfibre or lens-cleaning lint-free cloth
- A cleaning product that is safe and suitable to use on your phone
- A tumbled or small wand of selenite

What to do:

- Get your phone and sign in to your most used social media app.
- Spend the time you'd usually be scrolling to unfollow accounts that don't support your mental health. Either go through your feed or to the list of people and brands you're following and unfollow or mute accounts that aren't invited to your house party.
- As you tap the unfollow or mute say, 'Just as I wish well for myself, I wish you well.'
- When you've finished, apply the cleaning product to the microfibre cloth and wipe over the front and back surfaces of your phone.
- As you leave your phone to charge overnight, place the selenite on it with the intention that the mineral will help you to let go of any unwanted attachments to those you've unfollowed.

Optional: After your unfollowing session, replace the existing phone cover with a new one. Choose it to represent how you want to feel when you're using your phone.

Burn, Baby, Burn

Don't put your life on hold for someone who won't or can't give you the answers you want. Instead of waiting for closure, close the door yourself. Write to them. This letter isn't for anyone's eyes but yours. Write your heart out, say anything that you need to get off your chest and let it go. Burn it, bury it or shred it to be recycled. No matter how tempting it is: DO NOT SEND THIS LETTER. It's time to let go of believing that this experience defines you or is holding you back.

You will need:

- A candle
- Paper and something to write with
- Lighter or matches

What to do:

- Set up a sacred space (see page 17). As you light the candle, say, 'May I be supported to let go of what no longer serves me.'
- Write a letter to the person you want to let go. Begin 'Dear [insert name], I'm writing this letter as a symbol of my intention to move on . . .' Continue with whatever you want to say to that person.
- Make sure that you take responsibility for your role in the situation and you aren't just playing the blame game.

- Conclude with something along these lines or that reso-nates with you. 'Thank you for the good times and the lessons but now I'm choosing myself. Goodbye, [sign your name].'
- When you've finished, take a deep breath and imagine you're calling back your power as you inhale. When you exhale, imagine that you are letting that person or situa-tion go.
- If you're going to burn the letter, make sure it's in a safe and well ventilated space (ideally outdoors). Alternatively, bury the letter in nature or shred it to be recycled.
- As you light the corner of the letter, bury or shred it, say, 'I reclaim my power, now.'

DARK MOON
Old ways won't open new doors

Let It Go Ritual

You will need:

- A charcoal disc
- A small pair of tongs
- A lighter or matches
- Heatproof bowl or cauldron
- A white candle
- Pen and paper
- Dried rosemary (dispels unwanted energy, good for protection, new beginnings, blessings and purification)

What to do:

- Place the charcoal disc in the heatproof bowl and light it. You'll need to wait until the disc is glowing hot and is covered with grey-white ash before you can use it for the rosemary.
- Light the candle and sit comfortably in front of it. Close your eyes and take three slow, deep breaths, to help you

feel more present in the moment. When you open your eyes, bring your attention to the burning candle.

- After three minutes of gazing into the flame, ask yourself: what do I need to let go to create more space in my life for the things that make me happy and keep me inspired? Write the answer on a piece of paper. You can either continue making a list of what you want to release as a stream of consciousness or, if you need to, ask the question again. Write the answer that comes to you each time you ask. There are no right or wrong answers: trust the answers that come through to you. When you feel as if your list is complete, write over the list, 'I release this so that we can all be free.'

- Take a deep breath into your body, and as you exhale, visualize any chains breaking that have been keeping you trapped.

- In a well-ventilated place, where it's safe to do so, burn the piece of paper with your list. As the list burns, say aloud, 'I'm ready for a new beginning.'

- Take a pinch of dried rosemary and sprinkle it over the charcoal disc – it should be hot enough by now. Allow the smoke to wash over you, in the same way that you would with a smoke-reset ritual (see page 149). Visualize the smoke cleansing you of any attachments from the past so that you can move forward.

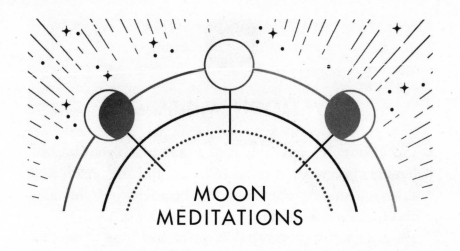

MOON
MEDITATIONS

These meditations can support you to align with each of the Moon's phases. You can do them on their own, accompany them with a Moon ritual (see pages 213–256) as part of a Moon ceremony (see page 198), before doing an oracle spread (see page 163) or spend some time journalling afterwards.

You could either read through the meditation to familiarize yourself with the script or use a voice recorder app on your phone to record yourself reading it so that you can listen as you guide yourself through the meditations.

Create a sacred space (see page 17). Sit up comfortably with your back straight and supported or lie on your back in a quiet place where you won't be disturbed. If you think you might fall asleep during the meditation, I recommend sitting up so you don't miss out on the magic.

NEW MOON MEDITATION

- Close your eyes and bring your awareness to your breath.
- Simply observe the natural movement of the breath as it flows into and out of your body to help slow your thoughts and quieten your mind.
- Extend the inhalation so that you're breathing in for a little longer, and breathe out more slowly.
- Bring to mind your new Moon intention and imagine it as a seed. Visualize planting that seed in your heart.
- Place your hand on your heart, and as you inhale, imagine that the breath is nourishing the soil for the seed to grow. As you exhale, visualize yourself blowing away any weeds or distractions.
- Take another slow breath, and as you inhale, imagine that the breath is rays of sunlight, warming the soil and activating the seed of intention that's in your heart. As you exhale, the seed begins to get bigger.
- Take another slow breath, and as you inhale, imagine that the breath is water that has nutrients to support the seed to get stronger. As you exhale, the seed grows roots and anchors itself within your heart. Soaking up the water through its roots, the seed of intention is ready to continue to grow throughout the Moon cycle.

- Spend a few moments in stillness.
- Bring some gentle movements into your body. Wriggle your fingers and toes. Stretch your arms. Slowly rotate your neck.
- Bring your hands together in the prayer position in front of your heart.
- Take one more slow, deep breath, in and out.
- Start to rub your palms together as if you were warming them, then bring your hands over your face, left hand covering the left side of your face, right hand covering the right. Open your eyes so that you're looking at your palms and slowly bring your hands into your lap.
- Ease yourself into the day (or evening).

New Moon Rituals, see pages 217–226
New Moon Oracle Spread, see page 165

WAXING MOON MEDITATION

- Close your eyes and bring your awareness to your breath.
- Simply observe the natural movement of the breath as it flows into and out of your body to help slow your thoughts and quieten your mind.
- Extend the inhalation so that you're breathing in for a little longer and breathing out more slowly.
- Feel your body relax.
- Place your right hand over your solar plexus (the space above your navel and below the sternum): this is the chakra that relates to your personal power, confidence, self-belief and self-worth. Breathe into your solar plexus, and as you exhale, visualize a fire burning in this space. Continue to breathe into your solar plexus, and each time you exhale, the fire gets brighter and stronger. Visualize this fire clearing the energy in your solar plexus of any self-doubt or limitations.
- Place your left hand over your heart and tune into its rhythm. Feel each beat as it rises through your chest and taps the palm of your hand.
- Ask yourself: 'What can I do today that will support my new Moon intention?'
- Observe and trust the answer that comes to you.

- Ask yourself: 'What can I do this week that will support my new Moon intention?
- Observe and trust the answer that comes to you.
- Ask yourself: 'What can I do this month that will support my new Moon intention?'
- Observe and trust the answer that comes to you.
- Take a deep breath and exhale slowly.
- Bring some gentle movements into your body. Wriggle your fingers and toes. Stretch your arms. Slowly rotate your neck.
- Bring your hands together in the prayer position in front of your heart.
- In your own time, open your eyes and reach for your journal to write down any messages you received during the meditation.

Waxing Moon Rituals, see pages 227–230
Waxing Moon Oracle Spread, see page 166

◯

FULL MOON MEDITATION

- Close your eyes and bring your awareness to your breathing.
- Simply observe the natural movement of the breath as it flows into and out of your body to help slow your thoughts.
- Extend the inhalation so that you're breathing in for a little longer, and breathe out more slowly.
- Visualize yourself outside in nature – this could be somewhere familiar or somewhere you've always wanted to go to. Feel your feet on the Earth and sense the temperature of the climate.
- As the Sun sets beyond the horizon, the full Moon rises above you.
- The moonbeams illuminate the sky and shine over you.
- As you observe your breath, imagine you're breathing with your emotions and anything else that's been coming up for you. Surrender to it all. There's nothing to change or fix. You're allowing everything to flow and giving yourself permission to be supported, now.
- Slow your breathing, and as you do this, imagine any emotional turbulence, confusion or overwhelmingness that you've been feeling calm down and quieten.

- Observe the space between each inhalation and exhalation. Hold the breath for a moment after you've inhaled, then exhaled. Follow this cycle of breathing for a few minutes.
- When you're ready to close this meditation: wrap your arms around your body and give yourself a hug.
- Take one more slow, deep breath, and as you exhale, release your arms.
- In your own time, open your eyes and ease yourself back into the day (or evening).

Full Moon Rituals, see pages 231–245
Full Moon Oracle Spread, see page 167

WANING MOON MEDITATION

- Sit down comfortably with your back straight and supported, or lie on your back in a quiet place, where you won't be disturbed. If you think you may fall asleep during the meditation, I recommend sitting up.
- Close your eyes and bring your awareness to your breathing.
- Simply observe the natural movement of the breath as it flows into and out of your body to help slow your thoughts and quieten your mind.
- Extend the inhalation so that you're breathing in for a little longer, and breathe out more slowly.
- Visualize yourself under a shower or waterfall and imagine that you're being bathed in pure white light, which washes over your head, across your shoulders and down your body. Allow the light to wash away any unwanted energy: any distractions, conflicts or attachments are being released as the light washes over you.
- Scan your body: if you notice any areas of tightness or tension, breathe the pure white light into your body, and as you exhale, imagine that you are releasing any blocked or stagnant energy. Visualize the light washing through your

body, radiating from your heart to the top of your head and down to the soles of your feet.

- Feel your body relaxing and getting lighter.
- Bring your awareness back to your breathing. Observe the ebb and flow of your breath as it moves in and out of your body.
- When you're ready, bring some gentle movements into your body. Wriggle your fingers and toes. Stretch your arms. Slowly rotate your neck.
- Bring your hands together in the prayer position in front of your heart.
- In your own time, open your eyes and ease yourself back into the day (or evening).

Waning Moon Rituals, see pages 246–254
Waning Moon Oracle Spread, see page 168

DARK MOON MEDITATION

- Close your eyes and bring your awareness to your breathing.
- Simply observe the natural movement of the breath as it flows into and out of your body to help slow down your thoughts and quieten your mind.
- Extend the inhalation so that you're breathing in for a little longer, and breathe out more slowly.
- Visualize gold roots growing from the base of your spine, down your legs and through the soles of your feet. Breathe in and connect with the roots. As you exhale, send the roots into the floor and down into the soil.
- As you breathe down into the roots, they get stronger, and as you exhale, they plunge deeper into the Earth. Imagine your roots spreading far and wide, taking up as much space as they need.
- These golden roots are secure and flexible, anchoring and supporting you.
- Say to yourself: 'I trust that I'm exactly where I need to be.' Repeat three times.
- Take a deep breath and imagine you're breathing all the way down to the end of your roots. Hold the breath for the count of three. As you exhale, become aware of your body.

- Take another deep breath, hold it for the count of three, and exhale for the count of five. Repeat four times.
- When you're ready to close this meditation: wrap your arms around your body and give yourself a hug.
- Take one more slow, deep breath, and as you exhale, release your arms.
- In your own time, open your eyes and ease yourself back into the day (or evening).

Dark Moon Ritual, see pages 255–256
Dark Moon Oracle Spread, see page 169

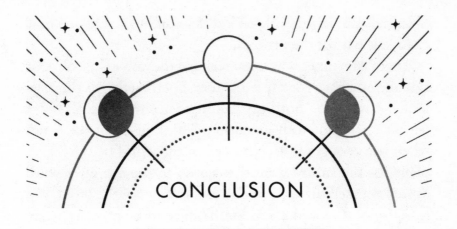

CONCLUSION

Getting to know the Moon is an opportunity to check in with yourself, take responsibility for what's going on in your life, and discover where you can make adjustments to align with the things that truly matter to you. Self-awareness is your superpower and when you start paying attention to your mental, emotional and spiritual well-being, that's when things start changing for the better.

There are times when change can seem scary – even when it's something you're actively pursuing. Sometimes the thought of our dream becoming reality is just as, if not more daunting than if it didn't. That's why we end up procrastinating and self-sabotaging, attempting to convince ourselves that perhaps being stuck in a rut isn't so bad after all. But the niggle doesn't go away. Deep down in your bones, you know there's more to life, which is probably one of the reasons why you picked up this book.

Understanding the Moon's cycles can help us to see how change is part of the process.

There'll be times when you feel as if the universe is on your side and you have your shit together, but then there's the existential crisis when nothing makes sense any more; it's also a necessary part of your evolution. Think of all of the times when you thought it was the end of the world because your plans for the future were thrown up in the air: after you'd dusted yourself off and put one foot in front of the other, you readjusted. A closed door doesn't have to be as scary when you know it's making space for a fresh start. I hope that this book helps you to feel more confident about embracing the unknown and perhaps even *excited* by the prospect of not knowing what's around the corner. Of course, we all love getting what we want but what if it's even better than you could have imagined? Don't hold yourself back by thinking the worst. Journal or use your Tarot/oracle cards to tune into what's really going on.

As you reflect on your motives, challenges and aspirations, you can move forward with your eyes wide open by cultivating a deeper sense of emotional intelligence. You may even notice a ripple effect as your interactions become more compassionate and your relationships transform, heal and start to feel more expansive. It's an opportunity to break the spell you've been under so that you can call more love into your life. The world needs more empathy, compassion, inclusivity and activism. Ultimately, we're doing this work so that we have more to give back.

We aren't supposed to have all of the answers all of the

time but what we do know is that change is constant, so you might as well get into the driver's seat. You could think of understanding the Moon's phases as knowing which gear to engage for a smoother ride.

This book is your direct line to the Moon's wisdom and support. You could think of the guide with the Moon signs (daily, birth, new and full Moons) as memos from the Moon letting you know what's up. The rituals and oracle spreads are a way to make the call to commune with *la luna*. The Moon is your mirror and can support you to detach yourself from any beliefs and situations that have been keeping you stuck. It's time to wake up. It's time to turn your challenges into opportunities for transformation. It's time to banish the 'shoulda, woulda, couldas' and get aligned with your truth. Use this book to get to know your process: what does and doesn't work for *you*?

Trust yourself.

You don't have to follow this book religiously: the Moon isn't going anywhere. Doing everything suggested in this book doesn't equal a fast track to enlightenment. There will be times when you're frustrated because you're convinced that you've done everything but you aren't getting what you want. The missing piece of the puzzle? Surrendering to the fact that you may not be getting what you want but you are getting what you need. Loosen your grip on how you think things should be working out for you: sometimes less is more.

Just because you think you're ready for what you'd like to manifest, it doesn't mean that it's ready for you just yet. You know what they say: a watched telephone never rings. The same can be said of manifestation. The key to taking things to the next level is being in harmony with your current situation. Aligning with the Moon can help you be more present in each and every moment and appreciate the blessings in disguise just as much as the ones you've been holding out for.

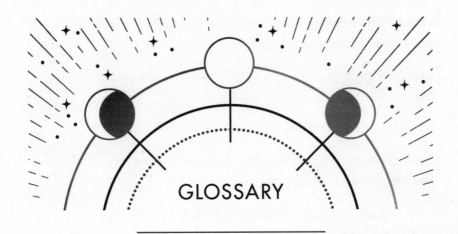

GLOSSARY

Aura. The energy field that surrounds your physical body.

Chakra. An energy centre; there are seven fundamental chakras associated with the body.

Divination. The practice of seeking knowledge and guidance via intuitive practices such as Tarot reading, palm reading, reading tea leaves and numerology.

Elements. There are four elements in astrology: air, water, fire and earth. Each element has its own distinguishing characteristics.

Emotional intelligence. Consciously expressing, controlling and having awareness of your emotions, as well as being able to handle interpersonal relationships, mindfully and with compassion.

Equinox. Occurs twice a year (summer and winter), when day and night are of equal length.

Grounding. Slowing down, feeling connected with your body and the present moment.

Law of attraction. Attracting situations and experiences, like for like.

Lunation. A lunar month.

Manifestation. Aligning with the universe to make intentions/hopes/wishes become reality.

Self-awareness. Understanding yourself, your motives, desires and fears.

Solstice. When the sun reaches the highest or lowest point at midday, these are the longest and shortest days of the year.

Surrender. Releasing attachment to outcomes and trusting the process.

Synchronicity. Meaningful coincidences.

Third eye. The chakra associated with intuition and perception.

Zodiac season. A period when a zodiac sign is aligned with the Sun; lasts about a month.